Hitler's

World View

A BLUEPRINT FOR POWER

By EBERHARD JÄCKEL

Translated from the German by
HERBERT ARNOLD

Foreword by
FRANKLIN L. FORD

D0973676

Harvard University Press
Cambridge, Massachusetts
London, England
1981

Contents

Foreword

by Franklin L. Ford

The mind of a despot holds some fascination for almost everyone. There are instances, of course, where our curiosity meets disappointment. Louis XIV's thinking, as distinct from his bearing, represents such a case, unless the paradigm of baroque monarchy is in itself enough to interest the observer. One might add concerning Napoleon, at the risk of unleashing a storm of indignant fan mail, that while his hard, retentive intelligence doubtless helps to explain his conquests, it still leaves any but the most abject admirer with an uneasy sense that there is less here than meets the eye.

Nevertheless, the banalities and the whims of an individual whose grudges and hunches alone could mean life or death to countless people will always command at least passing attention. If, in addition, the individual exhibits a degree of intellectual complexity, then something more is called for: an effort on our part to penetrate beyond idiosyncrasies and isolated actions to his or her view of the world and of the forces that move history. Surely no one would deny that such an effort is justified with respect to, say, Robespierre or Lenin. Can this be true even of Hitler?

Eberhard Jäckel's undertaking began with the knowledge that in many, perhaps most, scholarly circles an "intellectual history" of German National Socialism is

1

regarded as a contradiction in terms. He was equally aware that it has long been the fashion to dismiss as the boast of an ill-educated parvenu the Führer's self-congratulatory observation in *Mein Kampf:* "It may happen occasionally within long periods of human life that the programmatic thinker and the politician become one." Yet while this may have been a boast, Adolf Hitler believed it and in himself as embodying its fulfillment. That belief must be treated in turn as an important historical fact. For the apparent indifference with which he took such seemingly awesome steps as declaring war on the United States (not awesome to *him,* because the U.S. figured little in his long-matured vision of the struggle), the rigidity he showed in the face of mounting evidence that his miscalculation of England in particular was proving disastrous, these and many other features of his record remain inexplicable unless we recognize the mindset, jealously and consciously wedded to consistency, which lay behind them.

Jäckel calls attention to Hermann Rauschning's judgment, published in 1938 and quickly endorsed by countless other observers, that Hitler and his cohorts were bereft of real ideas, of underlying beliefs, and hence of any claim to consistency. There was, said Rauschning, no goal, whether foreign or domestic, that the Nazis would not glibly espouse or callously abandon in carrying out their "revolution of nihilism." Since the end of the Second World War, numerous historians and biographers have, it is true, expressed uneasiness over this dismissal of ideas in the history of the Third Reich, as well as over the paradox of denying the importance of Hitler's mind while at the same time conceding that the study of National Socialism is to a large extent, and necessarily, the study of Hitlerism. Such afterthoughts notwithstanding, however, a natural repugnance toward many of the ideas at issue and an awareness of the cynical opportunism so often revealed in Nazi *tactics* have combined to discourage most potential searchers from seeking the roots of what can reasonably be termed, for purposes of differentiation, Hitler's *strategy*. Both our author's approach and his method of proceeding have been determined by his belief that this distinction is as worthy of exploration as the strategy itself is of examination.

The result is a brisk, candid, and thoroughly provocative book. It is also what I think can only be adequately described as a "cool" book, in the sense that it is unimpassioned without being unconcerned. Jäckel's is not an attitude of moral neutrality toward the Nazi record or Hitler's central place therein, but the quest for historical comprehension would scarcely have benefited from endlessly reiterated expressions of disgust or indignation. Standing aghast is an unrewarding posture for anyone trying to pay close attention to the thread of history. Instead, we are invited to do what tragically few among National Socialism's eventual enemies and victims even attempted while it might yet have influenced the course of events. That is, we are given a chance to consider what Hitler thought, quite seriously and for a long time, about a number of very important subjects.

My first reading of this compact volume produced, if not pleasure at the contemplation of so baleful a subject, a stimulating awareness of having learned a great deal in a relatively short space of time. The writing is as crisp as the argument is lucid. The translation, by the way, deserves its own special vote of gratitude, for Herbert Arnold has succeeded in finding acceptable English equivalents for the most elusive products of German idealism and agglutination, *Weltanschauung* itself being one of them. He has done justice not only to the author's economical — one is tempted to say almost Gallic — exposition but also to the Führer's prose, at its worst a mixture of pulpit oratory, indulgence in a sort of journalistic hyperbole, and some remembered trappings of pre-1914 Austrian high style.

Without seeking to anticipate what the chapters that follow have to offer, I should at least point out that Jäckel's argument, indeed marked by lucidity, is by no means simple. It relies, to cite just one example, primarily on three documentary sources: the first volume of *Mein Kampf,* composed partly in Landsberg Prison and completed late in 1924; its second, and in some respects more narrowly focused, volume, written over the ensuing two years; and finally, the rather disparate but nonetheless revealing work of 1928 entitled *Hitlers Zweites Buch* in the German edition, *Hitler's Secret Book* in the English. This might suggest a perfectly sequential development of the future dictator's world view, but the author's treatment implies no such tidy progression. On the contrary, Jäckel points out the hesitations and ambiguities which yielded only slowly to the later, retroactive claim of "consistency." Similarly, Hitler's evocation of an articulated unfolding of his own experiences and ideas, from boyhood to the "Vienna years" to war service to the Party's formative period, is dismissed as either artful or, just as possibly, self-deceiving.

What is significant, though indeed far from simple, about all these uncertainties and tergiversations along the way is that in spite of them there does emerge a coherent outlook, twisted but nevertheless, by its possessor's lights, quite rational. In it the struggle of races for living space and the Germans' need to face up to the international role of Zionism come together in a definite set of aims and priorities, of inevitable national enemies and some "natural" allies. These calculations in turn culminate not only in a gigantic war but also in a terrifying "final solution" of the Jewish question, the latter seen not as the mad, self-imposed diversion it has often been considered, but as a strategic necessity, that is, *as an integral part of that war.*

In present-day Germany a debate is in progress between those historians who believe that too much has been made of Nazi personalities and, on the other side, those who insist that judgments must still be reached on the moral responsibility of the individuals who led the Third Reich. The two schools do not differ with respect to their revulsion toward such chieftains, least of all toward Hitler. To the "anti-intentionalists," however, excessive study of villains appears to trivialize the study of the National Socialist state, substituting demonology for the sober examination of conditioning factors such as bureaucratic structure, economic determinants, even luck itself in the timing and form of particular choices confronting the regime. To their opponents, on the contrary, any shifting of discussion away from personalities threatens to obscure the most chilling but also most important lessons bequeathed by twentieth-century German history.

It seems to me unlikely that Jäckel's contribution, or any other single volume, will resolve a disagreement so deeply affected by the participants' own differing *Weltanschauungen.* However, it may be worth asking oneself on which side of the argument his book will be seen as coming down.

Jäckel has certainly not sought to minimize the role of objective or impersonal factors that help to determine how even an autocrat must apply his general assumptions about the world to the intractable realities of one specific situation after another. Though he points out that his own emphasis is on ideas, Jäckel readily concedes that the work of others in examining how the Third Reich was in fact governed is of the first importance, not least when the actual practices are juxtaposed with the program in the mind of its supreme leader. On balance, however, by insisting that Hitler *had* a program, that he harbored not only hatreds and delusions of grandeur but also certain convictions, Eberhard Jäckel must give greater comfort to intentionalists than to determinists. In this sense, he comes out, it seems to me, not too far from the position suggested by Alan Bullock at the inspired close of his biography of Adolf Hitler. There Bullock translates the words of Sir Christopher Wren inscribed in 1723 on a wall of St. Paul's Cathedral — *his* cathedral — to the shambles of Berlin in 1945, offering them as an epitaph for Hitler: *Si monumentum requiris, circumspice* — "If you seek my monument, look about you."

Translator's Foreword

EBERHARD JÄCKEL'S important study refutes successfully the widely held assumption that Hitler did not have
a self-consistent *Weltanschauung*. It does so by a careful
analysis of Hitler's own statements, especially those contained in his two major written works, *Mein Kampf* and
his *Secret Book*. Jäckel's approach makes necessary the
extensive use of quotations from these and other primary sources. In order to enable the reader of this
translation to check for himself the quotations and their
contexts, it seemed appropriate to give not merely an
English translation of the individual passages but to
retain the reference to the original German source materials and to provide note guidance to the standard English translations of the two major works used. Hence, the
notes referring to *Mein Kampf* and to *Hitlers Zweites
Buch* give first the pagination of the German texts as
used by the author, and then include in brackets the
page numbers of the major English translations on which
the quotations are based. The English edition of *Mein
Kampf* used here is the complete and unabridged, anno-
tated translation published by Reynal and Hitchcock
(New York, 1939); the English version of *Hitlers Zweites
Buch* is entitled *Hitler's Secret Book,* introduced by
Telford Taylor and translated by Salvator Attanasio,
published by Grove Press (New York, 1961). Most of the
quotations in the text are taken from these translations,

with some minor changes, and all the note paginations refer to them.

Some of the quotations from the English version of *Mein Kampf* had to be changed for this translation. The reasons are twofold. At times, the author includes only parts of quotations in his own sentences; this necessitates a word order different from that of the complete English sentences found in the translation, although the sense remains, hopefully, unchanged. The second reason lies in the apparently conscious decision of the translators of *Mein Kampf* to be as literally faithful to the German original as possible. The result is frequently quaint, at times unintelligible — neither of which qualities is exhibited by the German text. In such cases it was thought best to introduce minor changes in the English version or to provide my own translations, since readability and the integrity of the main source of this book seemed more important than consistency in the use of the available English translation.

A brief remark on some of the major terms and their translation may also be in order. *Weltanschauung* has been retained throughout. It is well known and established in English usage; it also carries with it so many connotations and is terminologically so imprecise that no single English term could possibly capture the range of meaning contained in the German word. It has overtones of ideology, of a tendency towards, but not necessarily a fulfillment of, a systematic, comprehensive view of the world; everybody may be said to have a *Weltanschauung,* yet it is highly individually specific and shaped in complex ways by the general views and ideas of the time in which an individual lives.

Other frequently used terms did not seem to offer the same difficulties. Thus, *Lebensraum* is translated throughout as "living space," *Persönlichkeitswert* as "personality value," *Rassewert* as "racial value," etc.

While these terms are by no means common English usage in all cases, they seemed specific enough to warrant this kind of treatment, while they are also unfamiliar enough to alert the reader to the fact that he is dealing with Hitler's terminology. The author's usage of *"aussenpolitisches Konzept"* provided some difficulties and is rendered variously as "outline of foreign policy," "foreign policy conception," "grand design," or "overall plan of foreign policy," depending on the context in which the term occurs in the text.

It is my hope that this translation will provide Professor Jäckel's important study with the broad kind of readership and scholarly reaction which it so clearly deserves.

I want to thank the author for his careful reading of this translation in manuscript form; most of his suggestions have been included and have considerably improved the final version.

Middletown, Connecticut, July 1, 1971   H.A.A.

Hitler's *Weltanschauung*

Almost always will he have to forego the acclaim of his own time but, if his ideas are immortal, he will instead reap the acclaim of posterity." The tasks of the programmatic thinker and of the politician are, therefore, very different and that "is the reason why a combination of both in one person is almost never found." [15] But, as the sentence quoted at the opening of this book put it, they may become one in extremely rare, exceptional cases.

Although that passage was, incidentally, a homage to Gottfried Feder, there can be no doubt that Hitler, too, regarded himself as the prophet of a new *Weltanschauung.* Why else would he have set out to write a book which, according to its preface, laid down the fundamentals of his doctrine "once and for all"? [16] Nor can there be any doubt that he shared fully the fate which he himself had predicted for the programmatic thinker: "He works . . . for goals which only a very few understand." [17]

For first his contemporaries, then posterity, and finally historical scholarship have never agreed as unanimously on any point as they did in their verdict that Hitler did not have any ideas of his own, let alone a self-consistent *Weltanschauung.* From the start, his great theoretical work was regarded as unreadable by friend and foe alike, and as time went by it became the least read best-seller in world literature. "Nobody took it seriously, could take it seriously, or could even understand that style," Hermann Rauschning wrote in 1938 in his book on the nihilistic revolution of National Socialism without a doctrine, a book which until today has probably exerted the greatest influence on all the relevant literature. [18] Rauschning's thesis is that there was no goal, be it in foreign policy, economic policy, or domestic affairs, "which National Socialism was not prepared to give up or propagate at any time for the sake of the movement." [19] Its only goal was, instead, "the total revolutionizing of all elements of order" and total rule for its own sake or for the sake of the rulers. [20] There was a *Weltanschauung*; it was not used, however, as a *basis for* but only as a *means of* political action; it was there to be manipulated and to be used to strengthen the Nazis' power. [21] Even antisemitism was nothing but tactics and an instrument of power, an *instrumentum regni*. In Rauschning's second and even more famous book, Hitler said he would not destroy the Jews for "then we would have to invent them. One needs a visible foe, not an invisible one." [22] It was this sentence by Rauschning which found particularly widespread acceptance despite the fact that the prediction did not come true. [23]

From these foundations there arose a highly peculiar and increasingly contradictory state of research on this subject. On the one hand, there is the thesis of nihilistic opportunism founded by Rauschning. Nobody has put it more bluntly than Harold Laski, who said about Hitler in 1942: "Having himself no commitments to doctrine, being, as *Mein Kampf* made obvious, above everything an opportunist to whom rational principle was devoid of meaning, he achieved power simply in order to maintain power." From this premise everything else followed in logical sequence. For the sake of power — not on principle, because he had none — Hitler employed terror; for the sake of power, he created the war machinery; this in turn led to war, lest his power might be reduced, and he continued the war "since peace would have been fatal to his retention of authority." [24] Even in Alan Bullock's still unsurpassed biography of 1952, we find something similar. Hitler was consumed by "the will to power in its crudest and purest form, not identifying itself with the triumph of a principle as with Lenin or Robespierre — for the only principle of Nazism was power and domination for its own sake." [25] And in his epilogue Bullock calls Hitler "an opportunist without principle," with a specific reference to Rauschning's *Revolution of Nihilism.* [26]

While thus principles, goals, and *Weltanschauung* were rigorously denied on the one hand, a rich literature on Hitler's ideology and that of National Socialism came into being on the other. Surprisingly, this approach did not even conflict with the earlier one, for it denied either Hitler's significance in the development of the ideology or the relevance of the latter's content. This thesis, too, could refer to forerunners contemporary with Hitler. Thus Edgar Alexander wrote as early as 1937 that Hitler did not practice politics but *Weltanschauung*; he intended to subjugate the world to his "new Mohammedanism"; this new *Weltanschauung,* however, was nothing but "the principle of hate" and the right to use any means [27] — a way of putting it with which even Rauschning, given his premises, might have agreed. In 1953, Georg Lukács arrived at essentially the same conclusion, albeit from entirely different premises. To Lukács, National Socialist *Weltanschauung* is nothing but a demagogic synthesis of the philosophy of German imperialism, the application of American advertising techniques to German politics and propaganda, an instrument of attack against "objective truth," devoid of content and open to any kind of manipulation. [28] Like Lukács, Eva Reichmann invoked Rauschning when she wrote that National Socialism did not constitute a coherent system of ideas, although "Hitler and his clique of leaders had occasionally a fairly clear idea of their political goals." [29] Their *Weltanschauung* was, nevertheless, totally subservient to these goals — not vice versa. This book advocates more than any other, Rauschning's thesis of the purely instrumental nature of National Socialist antisemitism, thus aligning itself, too, with the opportunism thesis.

Some more recent German studies on the *Weltan-schauung*, program, and reality of National Socialism differ only slightly from the above in their arguments.[30] They all share the conviction that a thorough inquiry, at least into Hitler's *Weltanschauung*, is not worthwhile since he did not have one of any significant scope. It therefore receives only occasional and highly cursory remarks. Thus, Helga Grebing asked in 1959 what Hitler's *Weltanschauung* amounted to. (Like most of the other authors she put *"Weltanschauung"* in quotation marks). It amounted to "nothing but a thirst for power and the desire to rule – the entire world; a rage to destroy – every order; hate – against the Jews who were felt to be superior; subjugation – under the eternal laws of nature."[31] In 1960, Edith Eucken-Erdsiek asserted in an essay entitled "Hitler as an Ideologue" – without, incidentally, providing any source references – that Hitler had declared repeatedly "that he did not have any ideology whatsoever. . . . What did he strive for? For all or nothing. In any case, he strove for the most extreme intensification of possibilities: rulership over the entire world – and if that was impossible – destruction; the holocaust of the world – Muspilli."[32] In 1960, Martin Broszat at least mentioned the consistently pursued territorial policies in the East and conceded that antisemitism was probably Hitler's only conviction based on his *Weltanschauung* (again the word appears in quotation marks) "which was not subject to opportunist manipulation."[33] This constituted a remarkable departure from a scholarly tradition of more than twenty years.

In 1962, Friedrich Glum pushed the convictions of this school of interpretation to an extreme when he virtually refused to even mention Hitler in his discussion of the ideology of National Socialism.[34] All of these authors had, however, something else in common, something which one might call a leap into intellectual history. After a brief critique of Hitler, they abruptly jumped to "the" National Socialist ideologues like Alfred Rosenberg or Gottfried Feder and continued from there to their forerunners in the history of ideas, starting with someone like Moeller van den Bruck and going all the way back to Gobineau, Darwin, Fichte, and many others. There is no need to dwell upon this in any detail in the context of our approach, for which it is only important to point out to how considerable an extent the study of National Socialist *Weltanschauung* has assumed it could do without considering Hitler.

Thus, the main dilemma confronting historical scholarship became the astonishing and increasing emphasis on Hitler's political and historical significance in the face of his supposed insignificance in matters concerning *Weltanschauung.* Disregarding the rest of his thesis, even Glum stated "that without Hitler the development of Germany would have taken a different course." [35] This opinion arose above all from the biographical research on Hitler, the result of which was again and again that Hitler was the dominant, decisive, even ultimately determinant figure of National Socialism. This opinion can already be found in Bullock's explicit rejection of the view that described Hitler "as the pawn of the sinister interests who held real power in Germany." [36] It received even stronger expression in the book by Görlitz and Quint, where it was stated that "National Socialism . . . was Hitlerism"; [37] and most unequivocally, in Helmut Heiber's statement: "There was and there is no National Socialism without Hitler. The two are identical. . . . Everything else is simply a misunderstanding." [38]

The biographers stressed increasingly that Hitler had developed certain plans and goals at a very early time, as early as *Mein Kampf,* and that he clung to them to his end, as Bullock put it, with "consistency and an astonishing power of will." [39] Such persistently pursued plans occupy a considerable amount of space in the biography by Hans Bernd Gisevius, the most recent to appear to date. Although he still writes: "In his eventful career [Hitler] was to produce not a single idea," [40] the same author says about *Mein Kampf*: "If one reads it carefully, one finds in it everything, literally everything, which this man has brought onto the world." [41]

It is quite obvious that the image which was developed in this way became more and more inconsistent. Opportunism and consistency seem to be as mutually exclusive as Hitler's insignificance in questions of *Weltanschauung* and his significance in political and historical affairs. Nihilism seems to be an uneasy bedfellow of purposive action unless (and this would have to be investigated) the goals were nihilistic – which in turn would have to be defined. Personal rule is not readily compatible with the idea that Hitler left the development of his *Weltanschauung* to others. And finally, all of the above contradicts Hitler's claim that he also was the programmatic thinker and prophet of his own doctrine. Some of these inconsistencies might possibly be resolved; but there can be no doubt that there is no complete agreement between them.

In 1963, Ernst Nolte, in his great study on Fascism, made considerable progress when he attempted to delineate, among other things, Hitler's *Weltanschauung*. [42] He was probably the first to state that "taken in its entirety" Hitler's *Weltanschauung* formed an ideational structure, despite all its limitations, which was "breathtaking in its logical consistency." It is significant that he raised two questions concerning his own study of Hitler to which we will return in detail later. The first question was: "Is Hitler to be allowed to 'take the floor' again so many years after his death, after the entire world was forced to go to war in order to silence forever the hoarse voice of the raging demagogue?" And the second one was: "Is it worthwhile, is it not after all misleading, to build a structure of ideas out of ideas which are not ideas at all? Are not Hitler's 'ideas' an aggregate of vulgar phrases lacking in both originality and discipline?" Nolte was justified in raising both questions although he went on to reject them, for they characterize the dilemma of the debate up to now. It was on the one hand too passionate, and on the other too fraught with value judgments, to permit a candid look at the realities.

It is only natural that the debate should have been passionate. Hardly anyone has ever antagonized, insulted, and abused the world as much as Hitler did. He sowed hate and he truly reaped it. But he also found triumphant agreement, and he left behind many a bad conscience. Both of those things are understandable. But it is equally clear that neither of them has advanced, nor could advance, a straightforward recognition or a true understanding of what had happened. Anyone who starts out operating with the vocabulary of passionate negation and moral outrage, be it that he either cannot or does not want to do it differently, anyone who continuously employs derogatory quotation marks, anyone who thinks that he has to distance himself from his subject in every line, anyone like that cannot really expect to understand anything. Hate still blinds people; and in this case, the case of a scholarly debate, it is not the hated but the hater who comes to grief. Of course, if Goethe's statement is true that one cannot learn to understand anything one does not love, then all serious research concerning Hitler has to be given up. But may there not be the compromise of sober analysis? The present study, at least, starts from the premise that a dispassionate presentation of Hitler is sufficiently unmasking to render superfluous the continuous use of any epithets of abhorrence. I intend to do without them, not because of some moral neutrality but for the sake of understanding.

Moreover, up to now the debate seems to have deprived itself of any success by the premature intro- duction of value judgments — which brings us back to Nolte's second question. There may certainly be a place and a warrant for judging that way. But it still holds true that scholarship, for its own sake, is better off if, initial- ly, it abstains from such value judgments. Whence do we derive, for instance, the law that a *Weltanschauung* has to achieve a specific intellectual or moral level in order to be recognized as one? And even if there were such a law, by which yardstick do we determine the necessary minimal level? It also seems that the discussion has been much too abstract. Nowhere do we find even an attempt to define concretely what is meant by "nihilistic," by "opportunistic," or, for that matter, by *Weltanschauung*. Does nihilism mean that Hitler had no well-defined, concrete conception of his goal at all, or is it sufficient that he had none which one could accept? Does oppor- tunism mean that he was free to take advantage of any situation or merely of many? And if so, where do we draw the line? The scholarly discussion has, moreover, failed to distinguish with sufficient clarity between var- ious persons. Much as it may be true that National Socialism was Hitlerism, which is by no means generally accepted, it remains at least theoretically possible that Hitler had one kind of *Weltanschauung* and other Na- tional Socialists had another. Hastily to infer the one from the other, or to work from the assumption that they are all one and the same, is to anticipate a result which is yet to be reached.

In the face of such doubts and questions, more of which could be enumerated, the present study is based on three other premises. First, it is limited to Hitler and is content to examine his *Weltanschauung*. That does not imply, of course, that more encompassing questions become superfluous – as, for instance, the questions of a National Socialist *Weltanschauung* or its intellectual sources. But the problematical nature of the debate up to now seems to demand above all an inventory of one specific point, quite apart from the political and historical significance of Hitler himself. Provided accurate results can be reached, additional questions could then be formulated with some hope of success, starting out from the foundations thus achieved.

Secondly, this study is based on the assumption that Hitler definitely did have a *Weltanschauung* in the narrower sense of the word, no matter how primitive or nihilistic it may have been. This is simply a question of definition. *Weltanschauung* is, therefore, intended to mean first of all and literally the way in which somebody viewed or views the world. Even the totally illiterate, the totally primitive, indeed even the mentally deranged have an image of their surroundings, a view of the world. We may often be unable to ascertain it. But if someone has left so many and such varied expressions of himself as Adolf Hitler, it must be possible to examine this material with the questions in mind: How did he view the world and man? How did he judge life and society in the past and present, and in the future? What kind of goals, desires, utopias did he harbor? And so on. For the time being, this is all that *Weltanschauung* in a narrower sense is supposed to mean.

Thirdly, however, this study goes one step further. It will take into account Hitler's claim to the role of programmatic thinker, and it will inquire whether he fulfilled that claim. That is to mean *Weltanschauung* in a broader sense. Its prerequisites are that the individual parts of the *Weltanschauung* in the narrower sense are brought together into a self-consistent system and that

they are related to each other and not randomly inter-
changeable. In other words, what is required is a not
fully defined but visible systematic and inherent coherence. One may call that a "world picture" in contradistinction to *Weltanschauung* ("world view"). What is
important is that the former is assumed to exist in all
men and under all circumstances, while the latter, the
Weltanschauung in a broader sense, remains to be demonstrated.

This inquiry is therefore directed at the content of
Hitler's ideas. It should be added, to prevent any miscon-
ceptions, that this will lead to only a partial view of
Hitler, a view only of his *Weltanschauung,* not to a view
of his political methods, his tactics, nor even his strategy. To exclude all this by the very way in which we
pose our questions does not deny, of course, that all of
this did have extraordinary significance in the case of
Hitler. For it was Hitler himself who drew the distinction between the programmatic thinker and the politician and who accorded the latter greater significance:
"Every *Weltanschauung,* though it may be right a thousand times over and of the highest value to mankind, will
remain without importance for the practical working out
in detail of a nation's life, unless its principles have
become the banner of a fighting movement. . . . The
transformation of an ideal conception of the highest
veracity, based upon a comprehensive *Weltanschauung,*
into a definitely limited, tightly organized political community of believers and fighters, unified in spirit and will
power, is the most significant achievement, for the possibility of a victory of the idea depends exclusively on its
fortunate resolution." [43] Hitler thought of himself as
both a politician and a programmatic thinker and to ask
only for the latter is to look only for a part of the whole
phenomenon. But that does not mean that to pose the
question in this way is to underrate the other and

certainly more important part. It is not a question of underrating; it means only that for the purpose of a partial investigation, one part is left out of consideration for the time being. That investigation, however, is aimed precisely at a better understanding of the whole Hitler than has hitherto been possible.

There is one final methodological point. How are we to pose the question of Hitler's *Weltanschauung*? The problem here lies in the fact that Hitler did not define it systematically and step by step; it may also have developed and changed. A simple inventory by enumeration would not serve the purpose of this study, quite apart from the fact that it would be doomed to failure by the sheer mass of material. Two books, innumerable speeches and documents, and finally his historical impact would have to be taken into account. Attention would doubtless have to focus on the theoretical writings but always with an eye on the whole man and on the life in which his *Weltanschauung* found its expression. Inasmuch as the final outcome is to be a systemization of the fragments which were, as a rule, presented in a highly unsystematic fashion, there arises also the question of the procedure of the inquiry.

Faced with these problems, it seems most advantageous to proceed for the time being along the lines suggested by scholarship up to now. The next chapter will therefore deal with Hitler's concept of foreign policy, which has already been treated most fully, if by no means definitively. The third chapter will depict Hitler's antisemitism, the importance of which has always been noticed; and the fourth chapter will pose the question whether we can discern any additional goals and concepts, be it in Hitler's writings, in his speeches, or in his political practice. After we have thus outlined his *Weltanschauung* in the narrower sense of the word, the question of his *Weltanschauung* in the broader sense of the term will be raised, and with it the problem of a discernible systematic and inherent coherence of the individual ideas. That will be done in a fifth chapter, which is devoted to Hitler's view of history. The final and sixth chapter will once again, in a wider context, raise the question of the development of Hitler's *Weltanschauung* and will summarize the results and its relevance for our understanding of history.

CHAPTER II

The Outlines of
Foreign Policy

EVEN the discussion of Hitler's political goals has had a hard time in the face of the thesis of nihilistic opportunism, of the emphasis on the instrumental nature of his politics, and of his acquisition and retention of power for its own sake.

For if, as had long been asserted, there were no such goals, then there was obviously no need to look for them. And if one did look for them nevertheless, one might even come under the suspicion of intending to add features of greatness to the tyrant's portrait. Once again it was British scholarship to which international scholarship was already indebted for its first full-scale biography of Hitler, which opened up an unprejudiced approach to historical reality. As early as 1952, Alan Bullock had perceived a considerable programmatic consistency. H.R. Trevor-Roper, an Oxford historian like Bullock and author of the masterly study of Hitler's last days,[1] resolutely went beyond this cautious beginning in his two slim but pioneering studies of 1953 and 1959.[2]

He turned critically against the opinion of those historians "who were so repelled by Hitler's vulgar, inhuman character that they simply refused to concede to him anything as positive as clarity of thought and purposeful actions," considered it a mistake to "infer a low level of intelligence from a low level of morality,"[3] and outlined an impressive picture at least of Hitler's view of history and of his goals in foreign policy. He was the first to state that his view of history had been firmly established by 1923, at the latest, and that it had found an "absolutely clear and consistent" expression in Hitler's acts since that date.[4] Trevor-Roper depicted Hitler as a man – political thinker and acting politician at the same time[5] –who had held a repulsive but nevertheless grandiose vision of world history, of the rise and fall of empires on this earth, and who had then decided to erect once again a great German empire by conquering the East. That had been the vision of his life, the *raison d'être* of National Socialism.[6]

Starting out from these suggestions, since then repeatedly corroborated by new source material, an increasingly lucid and largely datable picture of the genesis of Hitler's foreign policy and military ideas has begun to emerge.[7] According to this new view, Hitler began his political career after World War I as a revisionist, very much like the overwhelming part of the German public. But in using this term one must not overlook the fact that, strictly speaking, it is not entirely correct. For Hitler's revisionism contained special traits from the start. He demanded not the reappraisal but a complete abolition of the Treaty of Versailles, and the reconstitution of Germany with the boundaries of 1914. This type of revisionism was, moreover, not aimed at peaceful negotiations, but was violent from its inception. Thus Hitler said, as early as November 13, 1919, in one of the first of his speeches that have come down to us: "The misery of Germany must be broken by Germany's steel. That time must come."[8] A statement of September 5, 1920, makes clear that this meant not only internal violence but another European war: "We are tied and gagged. But even though we are defenseless, we do not fear a war with France."[9] From now on, war, for Hitler, became one of the most self-evident means for achieving political goals. These goals might change, but the means remained the same, like an axiom. Since the goal was a revision of the defeat of 1918, such a war would be directed, above all, against France.

But how was Germany, in its miserable position, to wage a war against the strongest military power on the continent, supported as France was by the powers of the League of Nations? Hitler knew all along that by itself Germany was incapable of doing it. Thus his interest began to focus very early on Germany's remaining opportunities for possible foreign alliances, along with a radical change in domestic affairs, that other precondition of a new German rise to power. But in view of the unity of the enemies' alliance, it was possible to gain allies of any significant stature only by detecting and utilizing the differences in that alliance. It did not take Hitler very long. As early as 1920 he observed the frictions between France and Italy which had already surfaced at the Peace Conference and later over the Fiume Affair. On July 6, 1920, he concluded: "For us the enemy sits on the other side of the Rhine, not in Italy or elsewhere." [10] And August 1 of the same year, he said: "Our basic demand is: Off with the Peace Treaty! To this end we must use everything we can, especially the differences between France and Italy, in order to win Italy over to our side." [11]

Thus the idea of an alliance with Italy, which was to take on such prominence in later years, made its first appearance in Hitler's thinking. Hitler, incidentally, never forgot this origin and referred back to it repeatedly in later years. [12] It is important to note that this idea was not motivated by any ideological similarities with Mussolini's Fascism; that was impossible, since Hitler did not even know about that kindred movement in 1920. [13] For him the politics of alliances was, moreover, always purely a question of power. The sole decisive issue was the Franco-Italian difference of opinion, which could be used to Germany's advantage only if one avoided at the same time any Italo-German split; and that in turn meant not contesting any longer Italy's possession of the Southern Tyrol. Hitler did not shrink from this conclusion, although it meant that he now broke with a significant part of German public opinion and even with his own party comrades. For the Party Program of the NSDAP of February 24, 1920, demanded in the first of its twenty-five points "the unification of all Germans into a Greater Germany on the basis of the right of all people to self-determination." Hitler disregarded this demand with remarkable independence: "Germany has to work together with Italy, which is experiencing its national revival and which has a great future. For this it is necessary that Germany, clearly and unequivocally, renounce any claim to the Germans in Southern Tyrol. All that claptrap about Southern Tyrol, those empty protests against the Fascists, only hurt us because they alienate Italy from us. In politics sentiments do not count, only cold determination *(Kaltschnäuzigkeit)* counts." [14]

The Italian alliance by itself did not amount to very much, of course. But at least it provided the basis for an outline of foreign policy which could be pursued further. Next in line among the European powers were the Soviet Union and Great Britain. It seems that Hitler considered both possibilities. But he rejected the former, although the idea of a Russian alliance could look back to the Bismarckian tradition and was soon to be picked up by the foreign policy of the Weimar Republic. On July 27, 1920, he stated: "An alliance between Russia and Germany can only come into existence if the Jews are removed from power." [15] This was a reference to the repeatedly expressed opinion that the Bolshevik revolution had brought the Jews to power in Russia and that, as a consequence, hunger, misery, and disorder ruled in that country. The Soviet Union did, indeed, not look like a very useful ally, but Hitler noted that fact with a certain regret. For the British, on the other hand, he had long held great respect. Despite the enmity of the war he said on December 10, 1919: "As a people the Englishman (sic!) has reason to be proud." [16] It was above all the British Empire which particularly impressed Hitler. [17] But how was England to be won over? No other alliance seemed more solid than the one between England and France.

It was the occupation of the Ruhr in 1923, from which Great Britain quite clearly dissociated herself, that alerted Hitler to a difference of opinion which might be exploited in this case too. At any rate, from now on the idea of an Anglo-German alliance keeps recurring consistently in his speeches and it is always based on the British policy of a balance of powers on the continent. Thus we hear on April 13, 1923: "For 140 years England has battled France for hegemony. They are old and bitter rivals and continue to be rivals to this day despite the fact that they have waged a predatory war together." [18] Since 1918, and especially since 1923, a French striving for hegemony had again become noticeable which challenged Britain's policy of a balance of powers. Therefore, Hitler argued on August 21, 1923, Germany should have responded to the occupation of the Ruhr by taking up arms. Then the world would have realized that Germany had regained her senses and "a reorientation of English policy would have been the first natural result, a result which would have been welcomed in London. Not because they love us. No, for the simple reason which has always guided England's policy, namely to re-establish more or less the balance of the continental powers, for the sake of its own security and peace." [19]

Whatever one may think of this notion of a war of revision against France with the help of an Italian and a British alliance, one can hardly regard it as completely vague and devoid of content. But Hitler had by no means reached the end of his thinking on foreign policy. In 1924 he decisively expanded and modified it by some ideas concerning Germany's relationship to the one major European power he had left out. He introduced into his outline the idea of a war of conquest against the Soviet Union. We will need more studies, some of which are already under way, [20] to ascertain how Hitler arrived at this crowning climax of his program. Up to now, the almost universally accepted view has been that this shift must have occurred during his imprisonment at Landsberg when he wrote the first volume of *Mein Kampf,* and that it came about under the influence of certain possibly geopolitical ideas which came to his attention. This view has always suffered from the lack of sufficient corroboration by sources or even by substantial arguments. No clear-cut model has been found, and no matter what one may argue against it, Hitler's idea has a certain undeniable originality. The more recent thesis that this change in conception goes back to a more or less logical extension of Hitler's previous thinking about alliances seems therefore more plausible.

The Soviet Union undoubtedly became of central importance as soon as the alliance with Great Britain was seen as desirable. What was to be the role of the Soviet Union in the grand design of foreign policy, or – more precisely and more urgently – what role should or would the USSR play in the suggested Franco-German war of revision? On this, as on many other questions, Hitler went back to German diplomacy before World War I. Still undecided, he wrote in an article, which appeared in April, 1924, "In foreign policy Germany had to make a choice. Either one opted for winning farm land, giving up maritime trade and colonies, giving up overindustrialization, etc., in which case the German government had to realize that this could only be achieved in league with England and against Russia. Or one opted for sea power and world trade, in which case the only alternative was an alliance with Russia against England." [21] For the time being Hitler merely criticized the fact that "neither of the two" had been done, and left open other alternatives.

It is noteworthy that this choice between sea power and farm land (as Hitler elaborated, "to gain new land for the annual surplus in population growth") obviously pushed into the background or overshadowed with a wider perspective the previously advocated policy of revisionism. Hitler did not make a choice at this point, but with the slogan about the farm land he picked up once again a motif which had already made an occasional appearance in his earlier speeches. Thus, for instance, he had asked as early as December 10, 1919, whether it was right "that there is eighteen times more land per head for every Russian than there is for a German." [22] And on April 17, 1923, he had demanded "land *(Grund und Boden)* for feeding our nation." [23] But the expression remained vague, and so above all did the question of how and where that territory was to be acquired. Hitler's thinking about alliances seems to have brought him back to these ideas. If, as he seemed to suggest, one had to choose between England and Russia, then one had to or one might apparently also choose, as a necessary consequence, between either continental and territorial or maritime and commercial expansion. Within the framework of the general design up to now, one had to take Russia into consideration in either case. But this immediately raised the question of alternative goals and beyond that the question of what was to happen to France. Considering the complexity of the problem it seems inadvisable, probably even hopeless, to press too hard in a quest for the exact date and the motivation of this shift in Hitler's thinking which occurred in 1924. In all likelihood numerous and diverse considerations came together. It is much more important to keep in mind the solution which Hitler found. Historical scholarship has been familiar with it for some time.

That solution was presented in its final shape in the first volume of *Mein Kampf,* which appeared on July 18, 1925, seven months after Hitler's release from prison. Hitler had opted for the farm land solution and, once again, for the alliance with Great Britain. It is very suggestive that he mentions on the very first page of his book "the moral right to acquire foreign soil and territory," and he continues: "The sword is then the plow, and from the tears of war there grows the daily bread of generations to come." [24] This was further elaborated in Chapter IV. The starting point was a very simple fact: "Germany has an annual increase in population of almost 900,000 souls." [25] Feeding "this army of new citizens" was bound to become increasingly difficult and to lead in the end to a "hunger-pauperization," unless one took corrective measures. There were four possible ways to that end: birth control, internal colonization, expansion of export industries, or "the acquisition of new land and soil." Hitler rejected the first three possibilities and opted for the fourth one, the territorial policy. He added: "Obviously, such a territorial policy, however, cannot find its fulfillment in the Cameroons, for example, but almost exclusively only in Europe." Hitler also mentioned where: "If one wanted land and soil in Europe, then, by and large, this could only have been done at Russia's expense, and then the new *Reich* would again have to start marching along the road of the knights of the orders of former times to provide, with the help of the German sword, the soil for the plow and the daily bread for the nation." There was only one possible ally in Europe for such a policy and that was, of course, England. "To gain England's favor, no sacrifice should have been too great. One should have renounced colonies and sea power and spared British industry our competition." Even the German navy should have been given up and its place should have been taken by a "concentration of the State's entire means of power in the army on land."

The alternatives had been clearly spelled out. They lay between Russia and England, territorial policy and world trade, land power and sea power, but the grand design as a whole had gained very little in lucidity. It is relatively unimportant that Hitler once again cast all of his remarks in the form of a critique of German prewar policy, since he no longer disguised the fact that he had made up his mind. But what about the war of revision against France, what about the Italian alliance? How should or would France react in the case of a war of conquest against Russia, undertaken with the connivance of England? On all these questions the first volume of *Mein Kampf* remains silent, and it almost seems as if Hitler had been so overwhelmed by the discovery of the Anglo-Russian alternative that he practically forgot about his previous grand design. It seems even more likely, however, that the conflict between the two de-signs developed so far — on the one hand a war of revision against France with the backing of Italy and Britain, and on the other hand a war of conquest against Russia backed by Britain — still remained unresolved and that Hitler had not yet found a solution to this problem. Obviously, France would once again become central to his thinking.

That occurred in the second volume of *Mein Kampf.* Hitler worked on it in 1925, and the relevant thirteenth chapter, entitled "German Policy of Alliance after the War," seemed so important to him that he published it earlier as a pamphlet with a foreword signed on February 12, 1926. [26] Here, the proper goal of German policy was once again the "strengthening of continental power by the winning of new soil and territory in Europe"; [27] the means were war and alliances, the potential allies, England and Italy. "France is and remains the implacable mortal foe of the German people." Russia is not even mentioned. Had Hitler returned to the old 1923 idea of revisionism? That view seems to be contradicted by the retention of the territorial policy, but it finds support in the heavy emphasis placed on the Franco-German and Franco-British conflicts of interest, an emphasis almost totally absent from Volume One. The solution to this problem may well lie in the following sentence: "Today, however, we are not fighting for our position as a world power, but we must struggle for the existence of our fatherland, our national unity, and for the daily bread of our children." The emphasis is obviously on "today"; in other words, this chapter contains only the short-range program. [28]

The long-range goals, on the other hand, were developed in Chapter XIV under the title "Eastern Orientation or Eastern Policy." This chapter, too, was originally intended for separate publication — which, however, for reasons unknown and perhaps having to do with the publisher, never came about. Thus it was published only in Volume Two of *Mein Kampf* on December 11, 1926. [29] For Hitler's concept of foreign policy, this chapter is most important, since it contains for the first time all the previous components and their combination. Now Russia once again dominates. Germany's relationship to her was "the most important foreign policy question," [30] for the most important goal of National Socialist foreign policy was "to assemble our people and its might for a march forward on that road which leads out of the present limitation of the living space *(Lebens-raum)* of this people and on to new soil and territory." In other words, the goal is "to eliminate the discrepancy between our population and our territory – the latter viewed not only as a source of nourishment but also as a basis of support for power politics." But this time the war of revision was not forgotten, it was rejected outright: "The demand for the re-establishment of the frontiers of the year 1914 is political nonsense of such a magnitude and consequence as to almost make it appear criminal." For those frontiers were illogical, irrational, and unsuitable from the point of view of military policy, and they were above all too confining. To wage another war for them (for "only with blood" could they be reconstituted) "would not pay, by God." The only action "which, before God and our German posterity, would seem to justify an investment of blood" was "to secure for the German people the soil and territory to which it is entitled on this earth."

Thus the revisionism advocated since 1919 had been given up in favor of the much more encompassing policy of territorial acquisition. Since war was inevitable anyway, it should at least be worth while. Neither was France left out this time. Giving up revisionism by no means entailed giving up the idea, long advocated, of a military showdown with that country. Such a conflict would, however, remain "in the long range" ineffective "if our foreign policy aims were restricted to this war. It has and will retain significance only if it provides the cover for our back which is necessary for the enlargement of our people's living space in Europe." In the next chapter, Hitler insisted that "the long and in itself fruitless struggle between us and France" was only meaningful "provided, Germany really regards the destruction of France solely as a means for subsequently and finally giving our people the chance for a possible expansion

37

elsewhere." [31] That elsewhere was of course Russia, since "if we talk today about new soil and territory in Europe we must think primarily only of Russia and its vassal border states." The war of conquest against Russia would be a relatively simple undertaking: "The gigantic empire in the East is ready to collapse." [32] In Hitler's view, the October Revolution had been nothing but a change of rulers over the Slav masses, who were incapable of political creativity in any case; the previously Germanic ruling group had been replaced and exterminated by a Jewish one. But Jews could neither organize nor maintain a state. Hitler therefore concluded: "We have been chosen by Fate to be the witnesses of a catastrophe which will be the most powerful substantiation of the correctness of the folkish theory of race." [33]

But even under these new and different circumstances Germany would still be in need of allies. Once again, Hitler mentions England and Italy and refers back to the previous chapter of his book. There he had stated that the fates of different nations were "solidly welded together only by the expectation of a shared triumph, in the sense of common acquisitions and conquests, in short, of a joint expansion to their power." [34] That did not imply that Great Britain and Italy were, for instance, to have a share in a conquest of Russian soil. The new Triple Alliance was based instead on the assumption that the three partners would expand in different directions: Germany towards the continental East, England overseas, and Italy in the Mediterranean. Their interests were compatible precisely because none of the powers would interfere with any one of the others in the course of its own expansion. To facilitate matters, Germany would give up the Southern Tyrol to Italy; and it had to avoid, above all, any rivalry with England overseas. The main advantage of these alliances would be the isolation of France. After its subjugation, the "Eastern Policy" could be initiated "in the sense of acquiring the necessary soil for our German poeple." [35]

In this chapter, Hitler had successfully unified into one coherent program all of his previous thoughts on foreign policy, namely Germany's relationship to the four major European powers, the territorial policy, the policy of revision, and even his racial policy. It was now organized into three major phases. During the first phase, Germany's internal consolidation and rearmament had to occur, together with the signing of treaties with Great Britain and Italy. That would isolate France and would simultaneously afford an opportunity "to make quite calmly all those preparations which, one way or another, would have to be undertaken within the framework of such a coalition for a reckoning with France." [36] During the second phase, the war with France would become a reality, one way or another. That would eliminate not only France's hegemonial position in Europe, but also the threat to Germany's back during its Eastern expansion; as a by-product of all this Germany would inexorably achieve the fulfillment of its revisionist demands stemming from 1918, at least as far as they could be fulfilled on the continent of Europe. During the third and final phase, there would take place the great war of conquest against Russia — which should be easy militarily by then because it would be opposed only by the disorganized country of Jewish Bolsheviks and incompetent Slavs. But politically it would be of absolutely epoch-making importance, because it would gain living space for the German nation for generations to come and it would at the same time provide the foundation for Germany's renewed position as a world power.

It had taken Hitler seven years to formulate this outline of a foreign policy. He had not proceeded very systematically but rather in the manner in which he

himself had characterized the art of reading. [37] Time and
again, he had picked up a "small piece for his mosaic"
here and there, had assigned it "its appropriate place in
the general world picture," and had thus brought about
slowly a clearly arranged mosaic. It is important for the
course of this investigation to keep this method in mind.
Hitler's procedure had been unsystematic and he had
remained unsuccessful in his attempt to give to his
conception any systematic coherence. But he had another go at it. In the summer of 1928 he wrote another
book on "the fundamental National Socialist ideas of a
truly German foreign policy." It was never published at
the time for reasons which probably had little to do with
the content of the book, and was edited from Hitler's
papers in 1961. [38] Here the presentation was much more
successful. Perhaps his arguments had gained in coherence, as they undoubtedly did, precisely because nothing
had been changed in the general outline, new ideas made
only a peripheral appearance, providing some nuances,
and much of it was a literal repetition of what had
appeared in *Mein Kampf. Hitler's Secret Book* contains
the most precise and most carefully argued description
of his program which was now also incorporated into the
wider context of a view of history, to which we shall
have to return below.

Hitler's conception of foreign policy was now completed. It certainly was still riddled with contradictions
and absurdities. Were there not, for instance, conflicts of
interest between Britain and Italy in the Mediterranean
and in Africa which were bound to be detrimental to the
new Triple Alliance? Like France, Great Britain was,
without any doubt, opposed to Italy's expansion in
these areas; and they were supposed to become allies?
Moreover, was the Franco-British alliance not much
stronger in reality than Hitler assumed? Above all, was
his assumption really justified that Britain's policy of a

balance of powers made possible an Anglo-German coalition? History certainly did seem to teach that England had frequently fought against the establishment of a hegemonial power on the continent, and Hitler knew the relevant examples quite well.[39] But Hitler's plans amounted without any doubt to a German hegemony — indeed they presupposed it — and therefore had to lead necessarily to an Anglo-German conflict instead of an alliance if his premises were correct; quite apart from the fact that it was quite dubious whether France did indeed strive for a renewal of her hegemony in Europe.

Hitler at least recognized the dilemma but, in 1928, he tried to argue his way out of it with some peculiar and farfetched reasoning. Adding the only new idea to his previous arguments, he maintained in his *Secret Book* that it was most erroneous to assume that "England fought every hegemonial power in Europe immediately." Instead, history teaches that England does so only in order to eliminate competing powers overseas, but not as long as the goals of any given European hegemonial power were "obviously and purely continental in nature."[40] Consequently, even a hegemonial power in Europe might maintain an alliance with Great Britain provided it renounced any challenging rivalry overseas and restricted itself exclusively to the continent. Hitler was prepared to do just that; nevertheless, it remains very doubtful whether his interpretation of Britain's principle of the balance of powers was correct. Later on, as we know, it turned out to be wrong, and this miscalculation was to jeopardize the realization of Hitler's program more seriously than any other obstacle that stood in his way.[41]

In addition to these contradictions, which have by no means received an exhaustive treatment here, there were amazing omissions in Hitler's over-all plan. It dealt exclusively with the major powers and consequently never even mentioned how the war for living space was to be carried into Russia, considering that there was no common Soviet-German frontier. In other words, the later operations against Czechoslovakia and Poland had received no consideration in the over-all plan despite the fact that they were necessary first steps. The grand design also failed to mention how the Russian territories, which were to be conquered, were to serve for the settlement of German overpopulation, considering that they were already settled — and by no means as thinly as Hitler wanted to pretend with his use of dubious statistics based on the total territory and population of the Soviet Union. This gap in Hitler's thinking was to be filled in later by the gigantic projects of expulsion of indigenous populations, projects which found their expression above all in the so-called *"Generalplan Ost"* (General Plan for the East).[42] The frequently raised objection that Hitler had only insufficiently taken into account the factor of the United States, whose decisive role he should have known from World War I, is, however, not altogether valid. His thinking was based on the assumption that an Anglo-American conflict of interests would develop[43] which would prevent another U.S. intervention; quite apart from the fact that this intervention had also taken three years to materialize in World War I. But Hitler's grand design was doubtless one-sidedly Europe-oriented, and to that degree defective.

But apart from these and many other contradictions, absurdities, and gaps, disregarding also for the moment any kind of moral judgment, it can hardly be denied that this program of foreign policy already manifests a high degree of purposeful orientation, consistency, and coherence. Here we have clearly defined political goals and an indication of the means which might be used to strive for and possibly attain these goals. This certainly does not yet add up to a *Weltanschauung* as

Hitler himself understood the term. The system of ideas was still too fragmentary, still too much restricted to only one segment of human life, namely foreign policy. But would a mind capable of developing such a grand design not also be capable of demonstrating a similar kind of purposive drive and the gift of combining ideas in other areas as well? And might he not also have been capable in the end of developing an all-encompassing and coherent *Weltanschauung*? These are obvious questions, and they will have to be pursued further in the subsequent course of this study.

One thing at least seems clear already; one may call this opportunism, but as it has goals, it is not a nihilistic opportunism. One may call this power politics for the sake of power, but it has a clearly defined purpose beyond the pure wielding of power. One may call it lacking in principles, but it is not devoid of intelligible considerations of principles and tactics. One might say with Polonius that there is method in this madness, even though madness it is.

Having made this kind of judgment, the question becomes significant whether Hitler readily gave up or revised this outline of foreign policy for opportunistic reasons or whether he persisted in it. The answer is unequivocal. Even a cursory glance at the military and diplomatic history of the Third Reich demonstrates that this outline formed the guideline of those German policies which were defined by Hitler himself.

It is, of course, impossible in this context to undertake even a brief survey of the years between 1933 and 1945; there are a whole host of general surveys and detailed studies available on the subject. Up to now the entirety of National Socialist foreign policy has, however, hardly been approached consistently from the point of view of Hitler's over-all conception, which is unfortunate. Thus a few brief remarks may be in order, to point out some of the more important fundamentals and problems of the genesis of Hitler's foreign policy. [44]

In his inaugural speech of March 23, 1933, Hitler already singled out Great Britain and Italy from all other powers, by mentioning them with special emphasis. [45] After Germany's withdrawal from the League of Nations on October 19, 1933, had freed her from all multilateral ties, Hitler's first trip abroad as Chancellor of the Reich took him to his prospective ally Mussolini. But that *rapprochement* was delayed by the Austrian question. Instead, there came into existence the Anglo-German naval agreement of June 18, 1935, which simultaneously created a most important breach in the coalition of Versailles and was intended as a first step towards an alliance. But Great Britain remained averse to any closer ties, whereas the German-Italian *rapprochement* grew ever stronger from 1936 on. In this context the signing of the so-called Anti-Comintern Pact with Japan on November 25, 1936, was supposed to serve, as Ribbentrop stated in a fundamentally important note of January 2, 1938, as an attempt "to arrange Germany's policy of alliances in such a way that a German coalition would face a British one being either stronger than or perhaps on a par with it" in order to force "England to reach an agreement after all." [46] Wooing England had thus been replaced by threatening her, while the goal of gaining a free hand in Europe remained the same.

Hitler expected to achieve the same threatening effect from a number of political moves. First he established closer relations with Japan, to no avail. The occupation of Prague on March 15, 1939, led only to a British guarantee for Poland. This was followed, step by step, first by the signing of the Non-Aggression Treaty with the Soviet Union on August 23, 1939, and finally, when even that had not prevented Britain from entering the war, by the defeat of France. Just how much Hitler was guided in all this by his old ideas is shown in his explanation to Mussolini of the Soviet-German treaty. On March 18, 1940, he said: "As early as *Mein Kampf* he had stated that Germany could either go with England against Russia or with Russia against England. He had always intended to cooperate with England on the condition that England would not limit Germany's living space, particularly in the East." [47] Ribbentrop, incredibly, ordered that this reference to *Mein Kampf* be forwarded to Moscow for the perusal of the Soviet Government. [48] Their reaction is not known, but one can imagine the Kremlin becoming apprehensive when it learned that the Führer of the Third Reich still referred to that book which, after all, did contain a few other things about Germany's Eastern policies.

By the summer of 1940 France was vanquished, but Great Britain still refused to come around, contrary to all German expectations, despite her expulsion from the continent. Hitler faced the most important test of his policies and at the same time his gravest dilemma. He had now created all the preconditions for the great war for living space except one. Great Britain still would not accept German hegemony on the continent of Europe. At the opening of the Russian campaign, which he had already planned at the height of his triumph in the West and even before Britain had finally rejected him, Hitler was thus facing the danger against which he had always warned: Germany had to fight two major powers at the same time. But it was precisely this dilemma which led Hitler, in a most characteristic fashion, to devise a synthesis as a way out. During July, 1940, he decided on immediate war against the Soviet Union in the hope of achieving with one stroke an almost ideal combination of his two ultimate war aims, namely the final demoralization of Great Britain on the one hand, before the United States was ready for war; and on the other hand, the realization of his conception of living space. Once the latter had been achieved, Great Britain could no longer cherish any hopes; should she persist nevertheless, then Germany had a power base from which she could continue to wage war almost indefinitely. His dilemma even provided Hitler with an argument against his own hesitant generals. He argued that by eliminating Russia, one would also deprive England of her last sword on the continent.

The erroneous assessment of Great Britain turned out to be the decisive error in Hitler's equation and it continued to remain so. Because of this mistake, Hitler was forced to modify his grand design repeatedly, especially in the case of the Soviet-German Pact of 1939. But the grand design remained the lodestar of all his decisions in the field of foreign policy just the same. Few statesmen have ever pursued their goals with greater obstinacy or tenacity. One may continue to call his innumerable breaches of promises and treaties along the way opportunistic, but two things should be kept clearly in mind. This opportunism of cunning and lies was, first of all, one of principle. For Hitler, politics, as he repeatedly stated and as we shall see below, was a natural struggle for power fought according to the laws of the jungle. And secondly, this opportunism had clearly defined goals which did not at all arise from the opportunities offered by any given moment. They remained unflinchingly the goals and means which had been developed in the 1920's and which had been unified into a coherent conception of foreign policy by 1926 at the latest.

CHAPTER III

The Elimination
of the Jews

THERE was, of course, never any doubt that Hitler was an antisemite, either before or after his takeover of power and least of all after the mass murder of the European Jews during World War II. It is all the more surprising, therefore, that this most horrible of all the crimes of National Socialism has never been carefully investigated in the context of Hitler's goals and his *Weltanschauung.* As scholarship proceeded for some time on the assumption that he had no concrete goals, nor did he have a *Weltanschauung,* the result was a most self-contradictory view of history in this field too. Thus there is, on the one hand, Gerald Reitlinger, for instance, who opens his great study of the "Final Solution" [1] very late, with the Nuremberg Laws of 1935, if one disregards a few earlier incidental remarks, almost as if there were no need for an explanation of the fact that one day a state decided to exterminate the Jews as if they were vermin. On the other hand, there are the attempts at explaining German antisemitism in terms of intellectual history or mass psychology. The most important attempt of this kind is probably Eva G. Reichmann's *Hostages of Civilisation,* [2] to mention only one where Hitler receives relatively little attention. In this type of writing one frequently finds quoted Hitler's alleged saying which originated with Hermann Rauschning that he would not destroy the Jews. [3] This creates the impression that mass murder had not been, at least originally, one of his goals but had come into being as opportunistically as all the other points of the National Socialist program.

It is neither easy nor tempting to investigate for its origins and its possible motives something as antirational as antisemitism and especially Hitler's bloodstained version of it. However, considering the importance it had for Hitler's *Weltanschauung,* and considering the leading role he quite obviously played in that aspect of the Third Reich's policies, the gap between a description of National Socialist policies concerning the Jews on the one hand and the investigation into their historical genesis on the other simply has to be bridged sooner or later. But as long as we lack any preparatory studies and as long as Hitler's early statements are not available in their entirety, one can do little beyond pointing out, provisionally, some of the facts. This is attempted below.

There is, first of all, the fact that this point of Hitler's program can be documented even earlier than the beginnings of his outline of foreign policy. In a letter of September 16, 1919, which has been called the first written document of Hitler's political career, the conclusion of a lengthy discussion reads as follows: "Antisemitism based on purely emotional grounds will always find its ultimate expression in the form of programs (sic!). A rational antisemitism, however, must lead to the systematic legal fight against and the elimination of the prerogatives of the Jew which he alone possesses in contradistinction to all other aliens living among us (legislation concerning aliens). Its ultimate goal, however, must unalterably be the elimination of the Jews altogether."[4] The letter was written in answer to a question and the context of this correspondence makes it clear that Hitler was known as an antisemite even then within his own circle at the *Reichswehrgruppen-*

kommando (command of his formation of the *Reichs-wehr*) in Munich. It appears to be quite credible under these circumstances that, as he was to write later, he had become an antisemite even earlier, during his years in Vienna (1907–1913). [5] Even more important is the fact that this letter of 1919 already contains both central ideas of Hitler's antisemitism which were to recur again and again in some shape or another, later on: rational as opposed to emotional or pogrom-oriented antisemitism, and the elimination of the Jews. The latter was not clarified at all, while the former still remained remarkably vague. All Hitler had to say was that Jewry was "definitely a race and not a religious community," that it always remained true to itself within its host peoples, and that it was exclusively interested in money, material goods, and the fulfillment of its lust for power.

Ernst Nolte has pointed out that every one of the great ideologies of the nineteenth century contained its own brand of antisemitism. "Liberal anti-Semitism accused the Jews of antihistorical rigidity, intolerance, and 'national-separateness.' In socialist thought, the Jews often stood for the chief exemplifiers of the capitalist spirit and its 'mammonism.' What conservatives disliked most about the Jews was their spirit of unrest, their tendency toward revolution." Racial antisemitism had then combined all of these accusations into one and had traced them back to the unchangeable given fact of race. Within this spectrum of possible antisemitic accusations, Nolte assigns Hitler's antisemitism to the "radical-conservative wing." [6] These differentiations are important because they direct our attention to the appropriate kind of question. It is by no means sufficient to note the existence of antisemitic convictions in some general way. In the investigation of a *Weltanschauung,* the point is precisely to be specific, and thus the question becomes: Which accusations did Hitler level against the Jews?

Which in the present context leads us to a second question: What were the goals and means he strove for in trying to solve his problem?

The NSDAP's program of February 24, 1920, provides an unequivocal answer to the second question. It demanded that all civil rights for the Jews be abolished (Point Four), and that they be placed under the jurisdiction applying to aliens (Point Five). It denied them the right to hold any public office (Point Six), and it finally envisaged a series of measures concerning their deportation. Thus "members of alien nations" were to be deported if the entire population could not be fed otherwise (Point Seven). Moreover, additional immigration of non-Germans was to be prevented and those who had immigrated after August 2, 1914, were to be forced to leave the Reich immediately (Point Eight). Hitler's demand "to remove the Jews altogether" indubitably went beyond these points in the program. While he merely paraphrased the Party program in some of his speeches of 1920,[7] he was more radical on other occasions. Thus, for instance, he said on April 6, 1920, "We have no intention of being emotional antisemites who want to create the atmosphere of a pogrom; instead, our hearts are filled with a determination to attack the evil at its roots and to eradicate it root and branch."[8] Again and again he demanded the emigration or deportation of the Jews, which seems to define his meaning of "elimination."

On August 13, 1920, Hitler spoke in Munich for two hours on the subject of "Why we are against the Jews." It is the first of his speeches of which a complete copy has survived.[9] In his introduction Hitler warns once again against the danger of judging the Jewish question "on the basis of emotions" by distinguishing "good and bad individuals." He then goes on to develop a theory which is based on the concept of work and in

50

which he is obviously still heavily dependent on the
literature of antisemitism, a fact which could be substan-
tiated in this case in some detail. Whereas the people of
the north of our world, forced by the exigencies of the
cold climate, accepted the principle of work as a social
duty, the Jews understood work, as can be seen from the
Old Testament, as a punishment for original sin, thus
turning us all into convicts. [10] The former led to "purity
of racial breeding" and to "the strength to establish
states"; the latter, however, led to inbreeding (it remained unclear how this was to be distinguished from purity
of breeding) and to a lack of the strength which builds
states. Thus the Aryans had given birth to all the great
cultures, while the Jews had brought forth none of
them; Zionism itself was nothing but a farce. Instead,
the Zionist state was intended to serve the Jews only "as
the ultimate complete academy of their international
shabby tricks." For, like capitalism, the Jews are international. They preach the equality of all peoples and
international solidarity and it is therefore in their interest to de-nationalize the races. This is the first appearance in Hitler's utterances of that concept of Jewish
internationalism which had remained unmentioned in
1919 — although it should have suggested itself — and
which was soon to become the central accusation of
Hitler's antisemitism. (We shall have to return to this
repeatedly below.) All of this was accompanied by a rich
grab-bag of additional accusations, ranging from mammonism and materialism, all the way to the white slave
traffic — for which, according to Germanic feeling, there
was only one appropriate punishment: death. As the
goal for the fight against the Jews he suggested, once
again, a "thorough" solution, "the removal of the Jews
from the midst of our people," although it remained
again without any more specific explanation.

This speech contains almost all the themes which

were to be repeated and varied untiringly for the next three years until the Munich *Putsch.* But whereas, as we have seen, the outline of foreign policy had been continuously developed and modified during the same period, the conception of racial policies remained surprisingly constant. All the other charges notwithstanding, the Jews were, of course, more and more frequently associated with the adjective "international," and Hitler discovered more and more new areas in which the influence of international Jewry was operative. The revolution of 1918 and the entire Weimar Republic were Jewish: Marxism and the Soviet "dictatorship of blood" and, of course, high finance *(Börsenkapital)* were Jewish; the political parties of the Left were "mercenaries of Jewry";[11] and finally, democracy, parliaments, majority rule, and the League of Nations were all Jewish as well. But it still remained unclear what the goal of antisemitism, what the "removal" of the Jews was supposed to mean. On March 13, 1921, Hitler wrote in the *Völkische Beobachter*: "One has to prevent the Jewish subversion of our people, if necessary by securing its instigating virus in concentration camps."[12] But in a speech at Nuremberg, delivered on January 3, 1923, he said: "The internal expurgation of the Jewish spirit is not possible in any platonic way, for the Jewish spirit is the product of the Jewish person. Unless we expel the Jewish people soon, they will have judaized our people within a very short time."[13]

Only in *Mein Kampf* was this vagueness finally removed. Its two volumes repeat first of all, of course, all the antisemitic charges and goals of the previous five years; incidentally, in wild confusion. The events of November, the quiet of imprisonment or whatever had, nevertheless, led to a noticeable toughening and above all an intensification of Hitler's antisemitism. On the one hand, the eleventh chapter of the first volume, entitled

52

"Folk and Race," now contained a racial theory which, compared to 1920, had been considerably modified and expanded. We shall return to this point in a different context below since it goes far beyond the Jewish question in any narrow sense of the term. [14] On the other hand, *Mein Kampf* seems to provide us (and that applies to both volumes in equal measure) with four new aspects of Hitlerian antisemitism, namely its increased significance to Hitler himself; a new universalist-missionary element; its link-up with the outline of foreign policy; and, finally and above all else, an enormous radicalization of the intended measures.

As far as the first of these aspects is concerned, Hitler now made his antisemitism the center of both his personal and his political career. He calls his time in Vienna, during which he had changed "from a weakly cosmopolitan to a fanatical antisemite," the time of "the greatest transformation" which he had ever had to live through or, as he calls it elsewhere, his "most difficult change ever." [15] And one of the best-known passages of his book, a passage which is rarely quoted in its entirety and probably often misunderstood, reads: "With the Jews there can be no bargaining, but only the hard either—or. I, however, resolved now to become a politician." [16] Even if one takes into account that these two sentences at the end of Chapter VII of the first volume are separated by a new paragraph, which does not seem to be very significant, and even if one considers further the fact that Hitler was always very generous in his use of superlatives, there remains the fact, underscored by his other statements, that Hitler himself now regarded the Jewish question as the central motivating force of his political mission.

This mission leads us to the second new aspect. Hitler regarded it as an exclusively national mission and he passionately rejected any kind of international cooperation, even in the face of the Jewish threat which was supposedly so international in character. And yet in the antisemitic passages of *Mein Kampf* there appears at times a universalist-missionary touch which is absent from all other parts of Hitler's *Weltanschauung*. In Volume One he writes: "If, with the help of the Marxian creed, the Jew conquers the nations of this world, his crown will become the funeral wreath of humanity, and once again this planet, empty of mankind, will move through the ether as it did thousands of years ago." [17] He concludes: "Therefore, I believe today that I am acting in the sense of the Almighty Creator: By warding off the Jews, I am fighting for the Lord's work." [18] And in the second volume he states: "If Germany frees itself from this embrace [of Jewry], this greatest of all dangers to the peoples can be regarded as crushed for the entire world." [19] These aspects might, perhaps, neither attract nor merit attention if Hitler had not said something very similar two decades later when he was faced by his imminent military defeat. We shall return to this shortly.

The third aspect is concerned with so-called Jewish internationalism, which has now moved up all the way to the top of the list of Hitler's antisemetic charges, as is shown by almost innumerable passages in the book. "Jewish" and "international" became a virtually inseparable twin concept; only rarely do we find one of these words without the other. What is particularly new about this is the fact that in *Mein Kampf* this theory becomes linked with the grand design of foreign policy. That does not happen in the first volume, but it does occur in the second one in two important passages. One of them has already been mentioned in the last chapter above. It was Hitler's conviction that the war of conquest against Russia would be an easy undertaking since the Bolshevik regime was made up of Jews who, as we know, were unfit to build a state. The giant empire was therefore ready to collapse, and this collapse would in turn be the "most powerful proof" of the racial theory. [20] But if Jewish internationalism was an advantage for the future of German foreign policy in this case, it turned out to be a grave disadvantage in another case.

For in Chapter XIII, after the discussion of the future German policy of alliances, Hitler posed the question whether Germany was really acceptable to her prospective allies: "Is it at all possible for anybody to ally himself with present-day Germany?" [21] Three factors, he decided, argued against it. There was, first of all, the weak state of Weimar with which, of course, nobody would enter into an alliance. Secondly, in the countries of the potential allies there existed "a general anti-German psychosis which had been created by wartime propaganda"; [22] and there was, third, the influence of Jewry in England and Italy. The first two objections could be removed by a new powerful national government or by "years of continuous adroit labor," [23] but the third question was "the most difficult to answer" [24] and is the most interesting one in our present context. For the difficulty lay in the fact that in England and Italy, the Jewish forces might possibly have become so strong already that there the governmental powers could no longer serve the true national interests of these countries, which argued for an alliance with Germany. It was in the nature of Jewish internationalism to fight truly national politics everywhere. Thus it was in Britain's national interest, for instance, to ally herself with Germany. But it remained questionable whether London's Jewish world financiers would still permit such an alliance. In other words: "Can the forces – for example, traditional British statecraft – still break the destructive Jewish influence or not?" In Italy's case Hitler was rather more sanguine. For although Fascism did not fight Jewry directly, it fought at least against its three major tools: Freemasonry, the supranational press, and international Marxism. Thus there was some hope that the Italian government would increasingly serve the interests of the Italian people "without concern for the hissing of the Jewish world hydra." In England things were more difficult. There the Jew still ruled almost unchecked, and Hitler could derive only a certain consolation from the fact that even there an incessant struggle nevertheless took place "between the representatives of British State interests and the champions of Jewish world dictatorship." "The struggle against this Jewish world danger will, therefore, also start there." [25]

This combination of reflections in Hitler's antisemitism and his foreign policy is significant for two reasons. We are beginning to see, on the one hand, how he put together and interconnected the different points of the program which promise to be of significance for our question concerning the possible systematic internal coherence of Hitler's *Weltanschauung*. We shall come back to this point. This combination provides, on the other hand, some most valuable insights necessary for an understanding of Hitler's subsequent arguments on foreign policy. Especially after the alliance with Italy had been concluded and when it had failed to materialize in the case of Great Britain, which seemed to corroborate the theories of *Mein Kampf*, Hitler kept returning over and over to the explanation which he had first developed almost twenty years earlier. In numerous speeches and conversations he pointed out that it had been the influence of the Jews in London which had prevented an Anglo-German alliance. It is essentially on the basis of this background that we have to understand the untiring waiting of National Socialist diplomacy for a change of government in England and for a realization of what, after all, was in Britain's national interest. This also makes intelligible Hitler's profound hatred of Churchill, a hatred which contrasts so oddly with his respect for Stalin. But the latter, as opposed to his British colleague, at least recognized his own interests, and one could not expect that he would do anything but defend himself against the German attack. [26] As late as February 4, 1945, Hitler still deplored the fact that England had understood her own interests so poorly and that it had entered into the war against a Germany which had had absolutely no intention of infringing upon British interests; and in a fit of rare and, in this case moreover, unfounded self-criticism he added: "I myself have underrated one thing: the extent of Jewish influence on Churchill's Englishmen." [27]

Finally, the fourth new aspect for an evaluation of Hitler's antisemitism provided in *Mein Kampf* shows a downright monstrous radicalization and brutalization of the measures recommended in combatting the Jews. Hitler himself acknowledged this, by the way. On July 29, 1924, when he was asked in Landsberg by a visiting Bohemian-German National Socialist whether he had changed his position concerning the Jews, he replied: "Yes, yes, it is quite right that I have changed my opinion concerning the methods to fight Jewry. I have realized that up to now I have been much too soft! While working out my book I have come to the realization that in the future the most severe methods of fighting will have to be used to let us come through successfully. I am convinced that this is a vital question not just for our people but for all peoples. For Juda is the plague of the world." [28]

The previously advocated elimination of the Jews had now turned into their extinction and extermination; indeed, it had become quite openly an advocacy of their physical liquidation, of murder, while the old terminology was still retained at least in part. Hitler did not, of course, mean the physical killing of human beings every time he spoke of extermination. Thus he would speak of the "extermination of Germandom" in the Austro-Hungarian Empire, and the context makes it quite clear that all he meant by that was the "process of de-Germanization," a "policy of the slow squeezing out of Germandom." [29] In other words, one should not interpret his words too readily, nor should one always accept at face value Hitler's brutally strong language.

But there are numerous passages in which Hitler indubitably meant what he said quite literally, and those passages do not refer only to the Jews. Thus, for example, he wrote in the first volume of *Mein Kampf* that one would have to "if necessary, . . . proceed to the pitiless isolation of incurably diseased people; a barbaric measure for one who was unfortunate enough to be stricken with it, but a blessing for his contemporaries and for posterity." [30] Here at least the term "isolation" is still cautious although there could be no doubt as to the objective, but another passage in Volume Two was completely unequivocal. For there Hitler suggested "that some day a German national court will have to sentence and to execute some ten thousand of the organizing and thus responsible criminals of the November treason [of 1918] and of all that is involved in this." [31] It is plain that here we have the advocacy of murder and not of any due process of law.

In the antisemitic passages one is struck, first of all, by a very peculiar vocabulary. Here is a catalogue from Volume One of *Mein Kampf* as it appears there in the sequence of pages: The Jew is a maggot in a rotting corpse; he is a plague worse than the Black Death of former times; a germ carrier of the worst sort; mankind's eternal germ of disunion; the drone which insinuates its way into the rest of mankind; the spider that slowly sucks the people's blood out of its pores; the pack of rats fighting bloodily among themselves; the parasite in the body of other peoples; the typical parasite; a sponger who, like a harmful bacillus, continues to spread; the eternal bloodsucker; the peoples' parasite; the peoples' vampire. [32] Almost all of these expressions derive from the realm of parasitology; the Jew was isolated from the rest of human society, and the use of language suggests the methods of his elimination.

In his discussion of methods, Hitler showed no more restraint. War played once again a central role, as did the repeatedly stated conviction that the most profound, ultimate, and decisive reason for Germany's defeat in 1918 had been "the non-recognition of the racial problem and in particular of the Jewish danger." [33] If it had been recognized, then "the time would have arrived for proceeding against the entire fraudulent company of these Jewish poisoners of the nation. Now one should have dealt summarily with them without the slightest consideration for the clamor that would probably arise, or, what would have been better still, without pity for all their lamentations. . . . It would have been the duty of a concerned government . . . to exterminate without pity the rabble-rousers of this nationality now. While the best were dying at the front, one could at least have destroyed the vermin at home. . . . One should have applied ruthlessly all military means of power in order to root out this pestilence." [34] The war is important in this context; we shall have to comment on this later on. The war also provided Hitler with a special theory of humanitarianism: "When nations fight for their existence on this planet – that means when they are faced by the fateful question of 'to be or not to be' – then all humanitarian or aesthetic considerations dissolve into nothingness and disappear; because all of these ideas are not floating about in thin air; they come from the imagination of man and are tied to him. His departure from this world also dissolves these ideas into insubstantial nonexistence; for Nature does not know them. . . . Where a people's fight for existence in this world is concerned, all these ideas are of subordinate importance; they no longer have any decisive bearing on the form of this struggle at all if they threaten to bring on a paralysis of the struggling nation's force of self-preservation. . . . The most cruel weapons are humane if they lead to a quicker victory." [35]

What earlier had been vaguely called the elimination of the Jews now took on more clearly defined outlines. In Volume Two of *Mein Kampf* Hitler picked up this idea once more and wrote: "No nation can dislodge the fist of the implacable world Jew from its throat except by the sword. Only the united, concentrated force of a mighty insurgent nationalist passion can defy the international enslavement of the nations. But such a development is and remains a bloody one." [36] And he finally writes, at the very end of the book and more explicitly than ever before: "If at the beginning of the war and during the war, twelve or fifteen thousand of these Hebraic corrupters of the nation had been subjected to poison gas such as had been endured in the field by hundreds of thousands of our very best German workers of all classes and professions, then the sacrifice of millions at the front would not have been in vain. On the contrary, twelve thousand scoundrels eliminated at the right moment and a million orderly, worth-while Germans might perhaps have been saved for the future." [37]

One may or may not assume an association between the poison gas warfare of the First and the gas chambers of the Second World War, [38] but it remains certain that Hitler's antisemitism, as presented in *Mein Kampf,* contains warlike traits. It presupposes war, it demands the methods of warfare, and it is therefore not surprising that it should have reached its bloody climax during the next war, which was a part of Hitler's program from the start. One might even say that Hitler announced all that just in time. On January 30, 1939, when the preparations for war seemed sufficiently far advanced, he solemnly and publicly declared before the Greater German Reichstag in Berlin: "Today I shall act the prophet once again. If international financial Jewry inside and outside of Europe should succeed in thrusting the nations into a world war once again, then the result will not be the Bolshevization of the earth and with it the victory of Jewry, it will be the annihilation of the Jewish race in Europe." The minutes note at this point: "Long and vigorous applause." [39]

The Jewish policy of National Socialism can be divided into three major phases. During the years of peace the Jews were deprived of their civil rights and emigration from Germany was systematically enforced. With the beginning of the war, this was followed by a phase of deportation, the intended final outcome of which seems to have been the so-called *Madagascar-Plan* (Operation Madagascar), i.e., the deportation of the European Jews to that island which was supposed to become a territory under German mandate. [40] This could not however, be realized, and Hitler had already decided on a much more radical solution anyway. This third and final phase, the bloody so-called final solution, was initiated on a large scale in the summer of 1941, significantly at the very moment when the war against the Soviet Union, the final solution of the grand design in foreign policy, was undertaken as well. [41] In other words, the blueprints of Hitler's foreign and racial policy reached their respective climaxes at precisely the same moment. Indeed, there ensued a struggle between them about their respective priority.

In 1942, during the advance on Stalingrad, at the height of the Russian campaign – at a time, therefore, when one would imagine that the entire labor force and every means of transportation would be needed for that one goal — at that very same time long trains filled with Western European Jews rolled across Europe, almost according to schedule, to the extermination camps in the East. There the victims were murdered together with their Eastern European fellow sufferers at the very moment when the German front urgently needed every munitions worker and every piece of rolling stock. The logistics headquarters of the Wehrmacht and the *Reichssicherheitshauptamt* (the central security office of the SS), which was responsible for the final solution, tenaciously fought each other over the question of priority, only to be told that both were of equal importance for the war effort. In Hitler's *Weltanschauung* each of his two goals must, therefore, have been of an importance equal to or greater than the other; indeed, there seems to have been a direct connection between the two.

While the bloody deeds were done in secret, Hitler displayed a curious urge to talk about them in his public appearances, to manifest, as it were, his handiwork before the forum of history. During the deportation phase, he declared on November 8, 1940: "I have . . . again and again stated my view that the hour would come when we shall remove this people [the Jewish people] from the ranks of our nation." [42] Here the old term "remove" made one more appearance, but after the initiation of the final solution Hitler adapted his language to the new realities. In his New Year's message of January 1, 1942, we already read: "The Jew will, however, not exterminate the people of Europe; he will be the victim of his own machinations instead." [43] And on January 30, in Berlin's Sport Palace he said: "On September 1, 1939, I have already gone on record in the German *Reichstag* — and I am careful not to make any hasty prophecies — that this war will not end as the Jews imagine it, namely with the extermination of the European peoples, but that the result of this war will be the destruction of Jewry." [44]

Hitler repeated this pronouncement no less than three times in the course of 1942. On February 24: "My prophecy shall be fulfilled that this war will not destroy Aryan humanity but it will exterminate the Jew. Whatever the battle may bring in its course or however long it may last, that will be its final result." [45] On September 30: "On September 1, 1939, I stated two things in that session of the *Reichstag*: . . . secondly, that, if Jewry should instigate an international world war, for instance, in order to exterminate the Aryan peoples, then it will not be the Aryan peoples that will be annihilated but it will be Jewry. . . . Some time ago the Jews laughed about my prophecies in Germany, too. I do not know whether they are still laughing today or whether they have stopped laughing already. I can only assure you even now: they will stop laughing everywhere. And I shall be proved right with these prophecies as well." [46] And on November 8: "You will recall the session of the Reichstag during which I declared: If Jewry by any chance fancies itself able to bring about an international world war in order to exterminate the European races, the result will be not the extermination of the European races, but the extermination of Jewry in Europe. People always laughed about me as a prophet. Of those who laughed then, innumerable numbers no longer laugh today, and those who still laugh now will perhaps no longer laugh a short time from now. This realization will spread beyond Europe throughout the entire world. International Jewry will be recognized in its full demonic dangerousness; we National Socialists will see to that." [47]

This monotonous insistence is truly astounding and its motivation is not readily apparent. Did Hitler want to indicate to his accomplices in murder that he backed them with his authority? Did he want to have the final solution put on the record in time? Whatever the reasons, it is certain, at any rate, that he acknowledged his handiwork. It is also certain — and this is equally remarkable — that his dating of the "prophecy" as September 1, 1939, was wrong. It is true that Hitler spoke in the Reichstag on that date, too, but on that occasion he did not even mention the Jewish question. He undoubtedly referred to his Reichstag speech of January 30, 1939. It seems almost impossible that Hitler's mistake was unintentional, since he repeated it several times. The reference to the war may possibly have seemed premature to him later on. Whatever may have been the case, there is an obvious link with the war. The extermination of the Jews was a part of the war from the start. It is also significant that to Hitler the link between the terms "Jewry" and "international" was so compelling that it misled him into the nonsensical expression "international world war" twice.

The speech of November 8, 1942, quoted above, already hints at a return of what we have earlier called the universalist-missionary touch in Hitler's antisemitism. One has to remember that in the course of that autumn the second assault against the Soviet Union had failed like the first, and that the American invasion of North Africa had just begun. Yet, according to German plans, Russia was to be vanquished by 1941, before the United States was ready for war. Did Hitler begin to doubt the final victory? He would not admit it, but it now became obvious that the extermination of the Jews became increasingly the most important aim of the war as such; as the fortunes of war turned against Germany, the destruction of the Jews became National Socialism's gift to the world.

That became totally clear towards the end of the

war. In a conversation on February 13, 1945, Hitler said: "I have fought the Jews with an open visor. I gave them a final warning when the war broke out. I left them in no doubt that they would not be spared this time, should they once more thrust the world into the war – that the vermin in Europe would be exterminated once and for all." This now appeared to him as his central historical mission, for he continued: "I have lanced the Jewish abscess, like the others. For this, the future will be eternally grateful to us." [48] Hitler knew full well, of course, that he had wanted the war for twenty-five years, that he had planned, prepared, and started it. That war was now being lost, and yet not everything had been in vain. During his last weeks, Hitler stated that he had planted the best seed; he had been the first to tackle the Jewish question realistically, that was the merit of National Socialism and therefore – in Hitler's last words during his last conversation on April 2, 1945 – "the world will be eternally grateful to National Socialism that I have extinguished the Jews in Germany and Central Europe." [49]

After all his "prophecies" Hitler was not entirely wrong when he stood by his handiwork once more in his political testament on April 29, 1945, the day before his death: "But I have also never left open any doubt about the fact that if the peoples of Europe were to be regarded once again only as parcels of shares of these international monetary and financial conspirators, then that people too would be held responsible, which is the true culprit behind this murderous struggle: Jewry! I have also not left anybody in the dark about the fact that this time it would not only (sic!) be millions of children of Europeans from the Aryan nations who will die of hunger, not only millions of grown men who will suffer death, and not only hundreds of thousands of women and children who will burn to death in the cities and be permitted to be bombarded to death, without holding the true culprit responsible for his crime, even though it be by more humane methods." And thus the last sentence of his testament, Hitler's final word to the German people, reads: "Above all I pledge the leadership of the nation and its followers to the scrupulous observation of the racial laws and to an implacable opposition against the universal poisoner of all peoples, international Jewry." [50]

CHAPTER IV

The State as a
Means to an End

"The 'folkish' *Weltanschauung*," Hitler writes in the first chapter of the second volume of *Mein Kampf*, "sees in the state only a means to an end, and as its end it considers the preservation of the racial existence of men." [1] The conquest of new living space *(Lebensraum)* in the East, on the one hand, and the elimination of the Jews, on the other, served this purpose. Both served the preservation of the race; the former by securing its food supplies, the latter by securing its continued existence. That much our inquiry has yielded so far. The clichés of unprincipled opportunism and of the acquisition of power for its own sake seem already dubious to a high degree if we take into account the already apparent consistency which Hitler showed in his pursuit of these two ends. It would have been opportunistic, for example, to discontinue temporarily the persecution of the Jews in the summer of 1941 and to concentrate all forces on the conquest of living space – or vice versa. But Hitler was apparently no opportunist in this sense. He had principles, not moral ones, to be sure, in the usual sense of the Western tradition; but he had principles nevertheless, according to which his policies took their course with an obstinate, brutal, and finally self-destructive consistency.

One has to acknowledge, however, that even such a nonopportunistic consistency of principle does not yet constitute a world picture or a *Weltanschauung*. However one may define it, a *Weltanschauung* requires undoubtedly a higher degree of systematic coherence, of internal self-consistency than has become apparent up to this point. We have undoubtedly established certain connections and interrelations between the outlines of Hitler's foreign and racial policies. But despite these hints, there still remains the lack of a unifying system and of a synthesis of his individual tenets. Another question has to be raised, however, before we can answer this one. That is the question whether the two goals ascertained so far describe Hitler's program exhaustively, or whether there were any other points in his program which will also have to be taken into account when dealing with the question of his *Weltanschauung*. It is not only theoretically possible, it might in fact even be expected, that Hitler's program and thus possibly his *Weltanschauung* were much more comprehensive than the results of our investigation up to this point might suggest. To answer this question it is necessary to search for other possible goals and ideas, both in the practical politics of the National Socialist regime and in the writings and speeches of Hitler.

The Party Program of the NSDAP seems to offer an advantageous point of departure for this inquiry. It was promulgated on February 24, 1920, by Hitler himself.[2] From the start it was regarded as unalterable (Preamble), it was declared to be the "Fundamental Law of the State" after the seizure of power,[3] and it enjoyed the highest official respect until the end. But the Führer himself paid remarkably little attention to it although "the leaders of the Party," according to the final sentence, pledged "to support the execution of the above points ruthlessly, if necessary at the risk of their own lives." The first three points dealt with foreign policy. Point One demanded "the unification of all Germans on

the basis of the right of national self-determination."
Yet, barely three years later, Hitler went beyond it in his
renunciation of any claim "to the Germans in Southern
Tyrol." [4] Neither did he grasp the opportunity which
offered itself in 1940 of bringing back from Denmark to
the Reich *(heim ins Reich)* the Germans of Northern
Schleswig, much to the bitter disappointment of the
Germans in question.[5] Points Four through Eight of the
Program were concerned with Jewish policies. It has
been shown in the preceding chapter that Hitler went far
beyond them.[6] But his two most important goals, his
territorial policy and his antisemitism, still corresponded
to the first two major parts of the program at least
approximately, even if Hitler interpreted them very in-
dependently.

But he never paid the slightest attention to most of
the remaining seventeen points except where they presented platitudinous commonplaces. Let us briefly survey them in order of appearance. Points Nine and Ten
were vague generalities; one of them demanded the
equality of all citizens (which had already been severely
curtailed by the preceding points), the other emphasized
the duty "to work mentally or bodily." Both of these
points were, moreover, already covered by Articles 109
and 163 of the Reich Constitution of Weimar. Point
Eleven demanded the "elimination of incomes achieved
without work or toil," as well as the "breaking of the
tyranny of interest" *(Zinsknechtschaft)* – emphasized in
print. This phrase goes back to Gottfried Feder, and
Hitler in *Mein Kampf* calls it a "theoretical truth . . . of
immense significance for the future of the German nation;" [7] like its originator, it fell prey to well-deserved
total oblivion immediately after the seizure of power. In
1933 Feder briefly served as a *Staatssekretär* (Assistant
Secretary) in the *Reichswirtschaftsministerium* (Ministry
of Economics), but as early as 1934 he had to settle for

an honorary professorship at the Technical University of Berlin and remained without any influence after that. Neither was the realization of the demands contained in Points Twelve through Fourteen ever seriously undertaken, let alone followed through. They dealt with the "complete confiscation of all war profits," the "nationalization of all trusts [businesses] which have already gone public (so far)," as well as the "sharing of the profits of large concerns," whatever that may have meant. Point Fifteen, "Extension of Old Age Pensions," corresponded to Article 161 of the Weimar Constitution and was never regarded as urgent. Point Sixteen soon lapsed into total disregard as well; it demanded, apart from some generalities like the "creation of a sound middle class," especially the "immediate local socialization of all large department stores and their renting out to small businessmen at low cost"! [8]

There was no room in the Third Reich for any of these proclamations of a *petit bourgeois* version of vulgar socialism. But while it was sufficient on these points to spread the blanket of total silence over them, it became necessary even long before the seizure of power to alter decisively, if not give up completely, Point Seventeen of the unalterable program. It demanded an agrarian reform, including the "enactment of a law concerning the confiscation without compensation of land for purposes of public utility." This aroused such a storm of protests that Hitler was forced, on April 13, 1928, to "divulge" a declaration "against the mendacious interpretations" of this point, which declaration became henceforth a permanent, integral part of the Program. It stated that the NSDAP believed in private property and that the passage concerning confiscations was consequently directed "primarily against the Jewish companies involved in real estate speculation."

The remaining points of the Program dealt with

various aspects of domestic policy, and some of those at least were put into practice, such as, naturally, capital punishment for "common criminals against the people" (Point Eighteen). Point Nineteen, on the other hand, which demanded the "replacing of Roman law which serves the materialist world order by a German common law," fared much worse. There was no dearth of advocates for a regeneration of law through the spirit of National Socialism, but the regime never got around to any new codification, and it did not even promulgate the new penal code which had already been drafted. The last points of the Program, finally, concerned the further development of a system of general education (Point Twenty), the improvement of public health (Point Twenty-one), the creation of a people's army (Point Twenty-two), control of the press (Point Twenty-three) and freedom of religion (Point Twenty-four), limited of course by the "sense of decency and morality of the Germanic race." These demands were neither particularly original, nor did they prove to be inconvenient later on. Point Twenty-five suffered an almost paradigmatic fate: one half of it was followed completely ("creation of a strong central power of the Reich"), the other half was disregarded just as completely ("absolute authority of the central political parliament").

The entire Party Program can be divided into four parts; one on foreign policy (Points One through Three), one antisemitic (Four through Eight), one socialist (Eleven through Seventeen), and one general part on domestic affairs (Nine through Ten and Eighteen through Twenty-five). The first and second parts corresponded vaguely to Hitler's program, the third lapsed into total oblivion, while the fourth part was realized wherever it seemed fitting. But Hitler certainly never made the Program the fundamental law of his policy. One has to admit that it was hardly suited for that purpose, for it was nothing else but an enumeration of the *petit bourgeois* grievances and desires of the postwar period. The fact that Hitler paid so little attention to it has, nevertheless, led to questions about the part Hitler himself had actually played in its drafting. On the whole, scholarship tends to view his part as very limited, regarding the program essentially as the product of Anton Drexler,[9] the soon-to-be ousted founder of the "German Workers' Party" *(Deutsche Arbeiterpartei),* and assuming that Hitler's role had been confined to its first promulgation.[10] This seems plausible in the light of later developments (for why should Hitler have burdened himself with a program which he had no intention of keeping?), but it is in conflict with the fact, mentioned in the same literature, that Hitler belonged to the editorial committee which drafted the program and that he already exerted considerable influence in the party on other matters as well.[11]

This contradiction seems to resolve itself if we recognize that the question has been put the wrong way. In Hitler's view, the Party Program was anything but an expression of the political goals to be pursued. It was instead merely a means to the end of gaining and organizing followers, and thus to the creation of the preconditions necessary for realizing a *Weltanschauung* conceivably quite different in nature. When approached from this point of view, Hitler could, indeed he had to, yield to the grievances and desires of the day and of the masses. He therefore could participate in the drafting of the Program and its promulgation without agreeing with it. At any rate, that is the way in which he himself presents the case in *Mein Kampf.* He saw his "own task especially in extracting, from the abundant and un-shaped materials of a general *Weltanschauung,* and in molding into more or less dogmatic forms those nuclear ideas which by their clear delimitation are suitable for bringing together those people who pledge their allegiance to this. In other words: The National Socialist German Workers' Party takes over, out of the basic trend of thoughts of a general folkish conception of life, its essential features. It forms out of these, with an eye on practical reality, on its time and on the existing human material, as well as its defects, a political creed which then creates, in turn, by the tightly organizing integration of great human masses, made possible by this, the preconditions for the victorious fighting through of this *Weltanschauung.*" [12]

The sentence is long, but its meaning is completely clear nevertheless. A few chapters later, Hitler develops once again the same ideas. The twenty-five theses of the Program "are intended primarily to give the man in the street a rough picture of the movement's intention. They are, in a manner of speaking, a political creed which, on the one hand, campaigns for the movement and which, on the other hand, is suited for uniting and welding together those who have been attracted by a generally acknowledged obligation." The Program thus "had to take psychological factors into consideration." Its phrasing might well be improved, but any attempt of this sort would more often than not lead to disaster because it led to interminable debate and general confusion, which was not desirable at all. "For how does one think to fill people with a blind faith in the correctness of a doctrine if, by continual changes in its outward construction, one spreads uncertainty and doubt?" Nothing essential will, after all, ever be found in the externals of formulation but only in its innermost meaning. Anyone, therefore, who truly wished for a victory of the folkish *Weltanschauung* would have to have, first of all, a movement capable of fighting for this cause, a popular party "that does not consist only of intellectual leaders, but also of manual laborers." Such a party required, secondly, a program to which it adhered once and for all. "For the bulk of our followers, the nature of our movement will lie less in the letter of our principles but rather in the meaning which we are able to give to them." [13]

Hitler could hardly have underscored the Party Program's purely, or at least predominantly, instrumental character any more clearly than that. It was a means to an end. Under these circumstances it is rather insignificant how large or how small a part Hitler played in writing the Program or with how many of the twenty-five points he disagreed either at the time or later. He admitted that he did not feel bound by them in any way. He was free. This freedom was granted only a short time later, by his unlimited position of leader within the Party even in theory. One may call that opportunistic as long as one does not forget that it was a thoroughly conscious opportunism and one of principle and that, above all, this opportunism did not serve the acquisition of power for power's sake but the victorious march of a *Weltanschauung.* [14] We have thus gained an important insight which refers us back to the beginning of this study and to Hitler's distinction between the programmatic thinker and the politician mentioned there. [15] As a programmatic thinker he had to create a *Weltanschauung* which was true and ideal; as a politician he had to realize it, while taking into consideration what was humanly possible. The Party Program was one of the means to this end. Which leads to the linguistically paradoxical, but substantively unequivocal, conclusion that, where the Party Program was concerned, Hitler was precisely not the programmatic thinker of a *Weltanschauung,* but the political tactician. In other words, when approached in this way, the Party Program will not provide any answers to anyone asking for Hitler's *Weltanschauung.*

The above interpretation of the Party Program was worth while all the same. It has led to an additional clarification of Hitler's thought, and it has demonstrated that one has to turn elsewhere for any theoretical goals beyond the two already discovered ones of territorial policy and antisemitism, if such goals do exist at all. They will certainly not be found in Hitler's books and speeches. To the extent that they have not been treated already in this study, these consist essentially – apart from passages relating to Hitler's autobiography or to party history – of considerations concerning political tactics or of attacks on existing conditions in Germany. Considerations of tactics have absolutely nothing to do with the *Weltanschauung* of the programmatic thinker except with respect to the methods by which they are to be realized; these we have repeatedly dealt with and shall continue to deal with. The attack on the Weimar Republic, on democracy and parliamentarianism, on Marxists, Socialists, and so forth is, as will be shown, only a subcategory of Hitler's antisemitism in the context of his *Weltanschauung*. If we are looking for any of Hitler's additional long-range political goals of any substance, we will have to look for them in his rule and in his state.

His *"Führerstaat"* was a most peculiar, indeed monstrous construct. Hitler's constitutional policy limited itself to the development of a more or less effective personal rule. [16] He did not waste any time on providing his state with a new constitution. The old constitution was, however, at the same time neither observed nor abolished, which has raised the unanswerable question whether the Weimar Constitution was in effect between 1933 and 1945 or not. Not even the continuity of Hitler's state, the question of a successor – the central issue of any constitution – was ever settled legally. According to the so-called *"Führerprinzip,"* the Führer appointed every official, either directly or indirectly, while the way in which the Führer himself came into being remained without any explanation. This left no alternative to the Führer's appointing his own successor, which Hitler actually did in 1945. Side by side with the settling of politically unimportant issues on the basis of the old norms, there existed the extranormative realization of the true political goals via the so-called Führer orders. Under these simply chaotic circumstances, the attempt of the National Socialist constitutional lawyer Ernst Rudolf Huber to draft the constitutional law of the Third Reich in terms of legal concepts became, necessarily, a downright grotesque undertaking doomed to failure, considering the recalcitrancy of his object. [17]

Hitler was not interested in constitutional questions and treated them strictly from the point of view of opportunity. Let me hasten to add immediately that even this kind of opportunism was well thought out and was directed towards a specific goal. At the beginning of this chapter, I quoted Hitler's statement according to which the state, as viewed within the folkish *Weltanschauung,* is merely a means to the end of maintaining the race. In the second volume of *Mein Kampf,* one of the longest chapters in the entire book is entitled "The State." But it remains remarkably uninformative about its subject or about any problems concerning the constitution or the form of government. The Party Program had already been eloquently silent about the latter, despite the fact that it was, of course, a much debated issue in Germany after the fall of the monarchy, especially in a party which was simultaneously nationalist and socialist. In the first volume of his book, Hitler had stated that the mission of his movement was neither the founding of a monarchy nor the strengthening of the republic, but rather the creation of a "Germanic state." But he had failed to add even a word of explanation to this very vague term and had instead gone on to say: "The question of the external form of such a state, i.e. its final shape, is not of fundamental importance but is dependent only on questions of practical expediency." [18]

The chapter about the state in Volume Two pursues a very similar line of argument. It deals with the problems of race and the principles of education while avoiding studiously any formal constitutional questions. It does repeat, again and again, that the state is a means to an end. "Its end," Hitler says, "is the preservation and the promotion of psychically and psychologically similar living beings." [19] Or, equally vague: "Thus, the highest purpose of the folkish state is its care for the preservation of those racial primal elements which, by providing culture, create the beauty and the dignity of a higher humanity. We, as Aryans, are therefore able to imagine a state only as the living organism of a people *(Volkstum)* which not only safeguards the preservation of that people, but which by a further training of its spiritual and ideal abilities, leads it to the highest freedom." [20] For Hitler, freedom was never the freedom of the individual — it was that of the state; as it also is in this passage, i.e., meaning freedom of action in foreign policy. This clarifies the end of the state somewhat, as is shown by the following sentence: "The German Reich, as a State, should include all Germans; it has not only the task of collecting from the people the most valuable stocks of racially primal elements and preserving them, but also to lead them, gradually and safely, to a dominating position." [21] The state thus becomes a means to that end of hegemonial expansion which Hitler described with great precision in other passages. The shape and constitution of this state, however, were purely opportunistic functions of that ulterior end.

Everything noted above about the state also holds true for the entire realm of domestic affairs. In 1928, Hitler wrote: "Domestic policy must secure the inner strength of a people so that it can assert itself in the sphere of foreign policy." [22] Consequently, Hitler's own ideas on economic policy were dominated by a primitive, romantic agrarianism and by a striving for autarky, and both of them were subservient to his foreign policy. Hitler writes about all this in Volume One of *Mein Kampf,* significantly in the context of the first description of his territorial policy. "Industry and trade step back from their unwholesome leading positions into the general frame of a national economy of balanced demand and supply. Both are then no longer the basis of a nation's subsistency, but a means to it. Inasmuch as now they have a balance between their supply and demand in all fields, they make the entire support of the nation independent of foreign countries, thus helping to secure the liberty of the state and the independence of the nation, especially in times of distress." [23] These "times of distress" would, of course, occur during the period of expansion, and it is better that the state be free then, i.e. independent of foreign powers.

Such ideas could, of course, never be realized in all their purity when one pursued the policies of a major twentieth-century power, no matter how much the National Socialist regime would later on cultivate the peasant romanticism of "blood and soil." But that was not really the point. Even economic policy was, after all, not an end in itself but only an instrument, a means to the end of providing the state with freedom of action. Its details could be, and had to be, made dependent on considerations of opportunity. Thus the only genuine National Socialist theory of economics, the wild fantasies of Gottfried Feder, were abandoned immediately, as we have seen. Like the anticapitalist points of the Party Program, they had served only the function of advertising. National Socialist reality was ruled by a sort of guided capitalism [24] which, although not inimical to

the production of consumer goods, was primarily directed towards an expansion of heavy industry. This emphasis recommended itself for the sake of German arma-
ment, although this was by no means central from' the
very beginning. All of this was aided by Hitler's open-
mindedness in the area of technical problems, and especially motorization.

Social policies, too, came second to freedom of
action in foreign policy. Hitler himself wrote that he had
become significantly aware of social and economic questions only "as a consequence of my examination of
Germany's policy of alliances." [25] Considering the
theory and practice of National Socialist social policies,
one must keep firmly in mind one important principle
which Hitler expressed in these terms: "The first foundation for forming authority is always popularity. But an
authority based solely on this foundation is still extremely weak, unstable, and vacillating. Any bearer of
such an authority, which rests purely on popularity,
must therefore endeavor to improve and to safeguard
this authority by creating power. In power, therefore,
i.e., in force, we see the second foundation of all authority. This is far more stable, more secure, but not always
more vigorous than the first kind of authority. If popularity and force unite, and if thus combined they are
able to last over a certain period of time, then an
authority can arise on an even more solid basis, an
authority of tradition. If finally popularity, force, and
tradition combine, then an authority may be regarded as
unshakable." [26]

These sentences might have been written by Machia-
velli. Hitler took them to heart and followed them. The
one thing he lacked most was tradition, and he often had
to obtain it by tricks as he did on the "Day of Potsdam." [27] It has never been questioned that he created
for himself an effective machinery of power. However,

he ranked higher in popularity than in either tradition or power, and in the literature after 1945 that became, to use a pun, a most unpopular issue. Yet there can be no serious doubt about the fact that Hitler's regime was popular with the German people until late in the war. This is neither the place to corroborate that fact with the help of individual examples, nor to investigate how closely his popularity and power were interrelated. All of this plays only a minor role when one is interested in Hitler's *Weltanschauung*. But it has to be mentioned in the context of his social policies. [28] In *Mein Kampf* we read that "as far as tactics are concerned," and "in order to win the masses for the national uprising, no social sacrifices are too great." And that "the national education of the great masses can only come about via social improvements." [29]

That expresses everything essential. Hitler's own ideas on social policies were scanty and quite unoriginal. But that was not the issue. He needed the workers — first as "the reservoir from which the young movement will draw its adherents," [30] then for the "technical preparation" for battle, and finally for the "charging battalions." [31] He therefore had to "wrest" the "great masses" from the Marxist "delusion of internationalism." Little would be gained from "winning the common herd of bourgeois voters"; they only belonged to the "national camp" which one could only hope to "rearrange." The real goal was "to win over the anti-national camp. And it is this viewpoint which is ultimately decisive for the tactical attitude of the entire movement." [32] What Hitler called a *"Volksstaat"* (popular state), and what his social policies were supposed to bring about, was "a welding together of the people *(Volk)* to prepare it for war and expansion." [33]

With regard to that folkish-Germanic tissue of ideas on ideology and cultural policy which Alfred Rosenberg and others cultivated with such assiduity, Hitler declared repeatedly that he had a hard time perceiving anything concrete in it. He even had the refreshing ability to poke fun at it. "The concept of folkish," he said, was "not a possible basis for a movement." It was rather similar to religious faith, which is also "not an end in itself, but a means to an end; but it is the unavoidably necessary means for reaching that end at all. Its purpose, however, is not only an ideal one, but ultimately also an eminently practical one." Thus this factor, too, was assigned the role of an instrument. Hitler went on to say that the concept of folkish did contain "some fundamental insights." But they acquire value only "if they are integrated as the basic elements of a political party" and only "if the ideal urge for independence is provided with a fighting organization in the shape of military instruments of power, can the urgent desire of a people be transformed into glorious reality." [34]

We can now summarize the results of this survey. The state and all its aspects including the Party and its Program are only means to an end; an end, however — and this is absolutely crucial — which is very clearly defined, namely the realization of the twin goals of territorial policy and antisemitism which have become apparent earlier in the course of this inquiry. In other words, Hitler was indeed an opportunist to a considerable extent, and this may have led to the widespread notion of his total, unprincipled, and nihilistic opportunism. It has become clear, however, that we have to differentiate between total and partial opportunism, that Hitler's opportunism was definitely guided by principles, which incidentally were stressed again and again, and that it had a clearly defined content. Germany had to conquer new living space in the East, and it had to remove the Jews — and all the other aspects of public life had to serve as means to those two ends. Hitler's own expression about the state as a means to an end seems to be better suited, therefore, to describe the reality of his political long-range goals than the misleading concept of opportunism.

Both the theory and the practice of Hitler's rule are in keeping with this interpretation. In theory, it was characterized by the so-called Führer principle, i.e. Hitler's position first as the Führer (Leader) of the Party, and after a brief period of transition, also of the State; a position which was absolutely unlimited and responsible to no one, except to the imaginary idea of the *Volk* (folk). Both Party and State were nothing but instruments in the hands of the Führer for the purpose of realizing his goals. This leads to a total inversion of the traditional concept of state, since the ruler is now no longer the servant of the state but, on the contrary, the state is an instrument of the ruler. In practice, the Führer principle meant a total absence not only of any kind of constitutional or parliamentary control, but also of any system of collegiality even within the innermost circle of leadership. After 1921, when Hitler became First Chairman, the Party's executive committee did not meet even once, [35] nor were there any more meetings of the cabinet after 1937. Strictly speaking, there was no such thing as a common inner circle of leadership. There was only the Führer, extremely isolated even on the human level, and there were his extensions, appointed by him either directly or indirectly, on the various levels of the power structure. On the administrative level, this resulted eventually in a complex system of chanceries — each with a presidential, governmental, Party, and military function — which on the one hand passed along to the Führer all matters requiring his decision, and on the other hand formulated and handed down the so-called Führer-decisions, which were frequently oral. This entire system was based on a concept of absolute and hence irresponsible obedience which comes closest to the concept of following orders as it prevails in the military, from where it was probably derived. Everyone swore allegiance to Hitler's own person, not to the state. Since there were, however, no general political consultations except on questions of procedure, there developed a situation, which was most characteristic of this system and which could be repeatedly observed, in which even his closest lieutenants remained uninformed about the Führer's next moves, let alone the over-all goal of his policies. Alone Hitler planned, alone he decided (he declared innumerable times: "I have now decided . . . "), alone he ruled. [36]

We have found that his rule served exclusively the two long-range goals identified above. This brings us to the next and final question of our study. If, as it appears up to now, these two goals existed more or less side by side without any inner connection, then Hitler and his politics were clearly not guided by any consistent kind of *Weltanschauung*. In this case, Hitler would have simply taken over two ideas thoroughly familiar to his time, those of the territorial expansion of a nation-state and of racial antisemitism, and he would have attempted to realize them with an unparalleled consistency and radicalism. Or, to put it the other way around: if one is looking for Hitler's *Weltanschauung* in a broader sense, then one has to look above all for the possible fusion of his conceptions of foreign and racial policies.

Undoubtedly this kind of question must be directed primarily at Hitler's theoretical writings, which have already yielded a discernible programmatic consistency. It is, incidentally, the existence of such writings that should have prevented the rash assumption that Hitler, unlike, for example, Lenin or Robespierre, did not hold any comprehensive world view. The existence of theoretical writings is, of course, no proof in itself. But at the very least, they should have been thoroughly examined; previous scholarship, by and large, has failed to do this.

As a young man, Hitler wrote three theoretical pieces at two-year intervals. The first volume of *Mein Kampf* was composed in Landsberg prison in 1924.[37] In 1926 Hitler wrote the second volume, as promised, and in 1928 he wrote another book which was never published in his lifetime and which was only edited from his papers in 1961 under the title *Hitler's Secret Book.*[38]

The three books are very dissimilar in their organization. The first volume of *Mein Kampf,* subtitled *Settling of an Account,* is organized essentially along biographical lines, with each of the twelve chapters dedicated to the various stations of the author's life between his birth and January, 1920. It is, however, by no means a biography in the usual sense. The almost invariably terse autobiographical passages[39] are always followed, more or less artifically, by theoretical and programmatic reflections. Thus the fourth chapter, for example, contains only one single page about the details of Hitler's move to Munich in 1913, which is followed by thirty-two pages on foreign policy and the policy of alliances. Similarly, the sixth chapter moves from Hitler's war experiences to general comments about wartime propaganda. Chapter XI, entitled "Folk and Race," stands altogether outside the autobiographical framework.

As already indicated by the subtitle *The National Socialist Movement,* the second volume of *Mein Kampf* is organized in similar fashion around the history of the NSDAP, ranging in time from the promulgation of the Party Program in February, 1920, to the Munich *Putsch* of November, 1923. Although the history of the Party thus displaces the autobiography as an organizational principle, the result can hardly be called a Party history. Usually the presentation gives way very rapidly to general considerations and demands; six of the fifteen chapters are in this case devoted exclusively to programmatic and theoretical questions, including the two chapters on foreign policy, one of which could therefore readily be published separately and earlier in brochure form. [40]

The so-called *Secret Book,* finally, to which Hitler never gave either title or chapter headings and whose revision was never completed, arose from Hitler's desire to justify his renunciation of the South Tyrol, which had aroused a lot of criticism. The book therefore deals almost exclusively with questions of foreign policy, which are discussed at length and on the basis of fundamental principles; thus it contains the most complete and comprehensive account of Hitler's ideas on politics and *Weltanschauung.* Consequently, it also includes Hitler's reflections on his view of history as well as on his racial and domestic policies. The following chapter of this study will draw on all of this.

While the three works are thus quite different in their organization, they are nevertheless essentially congruous in their content, since they all reflect Hitler's political views either as a whole or in part. It is particularly significant for our approach that the two long-range goals which we have already identified are dealt with in all three books, and that they are — with the exception of a few, relatively unimportant nuances — dealt with in essentially the same manner. These repetitions, which apply also to a series of other questions, provide an important instrument of control for this interpretation, an instrument we have already made use of several times. Thus we have seen that Hitler's ideas, especially on foreign policy, underwent crucial modifications between 1919 and 1924. The three books written between 1924 and 1928, however, do not reveal any new major changes or differences, but merely more fully developed formulations or more thorough explanations of an essentially unchanging set of ideas. This interpretation may therefore neglect minor differences and treat the three works as a whole. The remaining difficulties are still formidable. The task is now to bring together into a system a multiplicity of scattered remarks which are on the whole presented rather unsystematically, although they are free of internal contradictions in all essentials.

CHAPTER V

The View of History
as a Synthesis

THE world of Hitler's political thought was heavily influenced by history. From the start he was fascinated by history, he argued historically again and again, and he had a considerable if idiosyncratic knowledge of history. His interest was anything but antiquarian, however. He wanted "to grasp and understand the meaning of history." [1] For him, "to learn" history was "to search for and to find the forces which cause those effects which we later face as historical events." [2] History, thus understood, became "an inexhaustible source for understanding the historical actions of the present, that is, politics." [3] For politics was "history in the making" [4] and, conversely, history was the "petrified representation of politics." [5] Consequently, history became "the most suitable teacher for our own political activity." [6] From history, Hitler learned "precisely the practical applicability for the present"; and he added, "But he who is unable to do this should not fancy himself as a political 'leader'." [7] Thus the politician, and especially the programmatic thinker, also had to be a historian and had to possess a view of history.

Folk or people and race are central to Hitler's view of history. He defined history as "the presentation of the course of a people's struggle for existence." [8] Put differently, "All the events of world history are but the expression of the racial instinct for self-preservation in its positive or negative sense." [9] The race question thus provides the "key to world history." [10] In other words, for Hitler, the bearers and the elements of history are peoples and races, not — as in other views of history — individuals, classes, cultures, or anything else. Thus, to give an example, Karl Marx had stated in the Communist Manifesto of 1848: "The history of all hitherto existing society is the history of class struggles." [11] Hitler, however, would maintain that history is the unfolding of the struggle for life or death of peoples and races, i.e. of ethnic-biological, not of social-economic groups.

Hitler used "people" and "race," as well as "tribe," "kindred," and "nation," as virtually synonymous terms. The following passage from the relevant chapter on "People and Race" in the first volume of *Mein Kampf* illustrates this fact: "But if it is ascertained that a people receives . . . the essential, basic elements of its culture from other races, . . . then one can . . . never call such a race 'culture-creating.' An examination of the various peoples from this point of view demonstrates the fact that . . . Aryan tribes . . . subjugate foreign peoples . . . " and so on. [12] In matters more or less theoretical, Hitler does not place a high premium on terminological precision. While this does, of course, render more difficult an analysis of his thought in terms of a system, it should not mislead one into giving up any attempt at such a systematic analysis or into the conclusion that Hitler's terms are devoid of meaning. Instead, a patient reading yields the insight that from behind all of his conceptual opaqueness there always emerges a clarity and comprehensiveness of content sufficiently strong to permit one to grasp Hitler's meaning; this is especially true if one includes in the analysis the graphic examples he cites.

Hitler's racial theory starts out from the principle of the "self-seclusion of the species of all living beings on earth." [13] By establishing an analogy between the realm of the animals and that of man, he becomes entangled in a downright grotesque self-contradiction. He argues as follows: "Even the most superficial observation shows, as an almost iron basic principle of all the countless forms of expression of Nature's will to live, her self-secluded forms of propagation and increase. Every animal mates only with a representative of the same species. The titmouse seeks the titmouse, the finch the finch, the stork the stork, the field mouse the field mouse, the common mouse the common mouse, the wolf the wolf, etc." Any deviation from this law is against Nature: "Any cross-breeding between two beings of not quite the same high standard produces a medium between the standards of the parents. That means: the offspring will probably be on a higher level than the racially lower parent, but not as high as the higher one. Consequently, it will succumb later on in the fight against the higher level. ... The consequence of this purity of race, generally valid in Nature, is not only the sharp delimitation of the races from others, but also their uniform character in themselves. A fox is always a fox, a goose a goose, a tiger a tiger, etc." After some further explanations, Hitler draws the practical conclusions of all this for man: "Historical experience offers countless proofs of this. It shows with terrible clarity that with any mixing of the blood of the Aryan with lower races the result was the end of the culture-bearer." And Hitler goes on to describe the difference between North America, whose Germanic population had mixed only very little "with the lower races," and Central and South America, "where the chiefly Romanic immigrants have mixed with the aborigines, sometimes on a large scale."

There is no need to comment on the nonsensicality of this kind of argument. It is common knowledge that white people can mate with colored people while a goose and a fox cannot mate with each other. By way of analogy, the principle of species-specific propagation is suddenly transformed from a law of nature into a postulate. At this point, the totally irrational and unscientific character of Hitler's racial theory, as well as almost any other one, becomes particularly apparent. His absurd argument reveals, nevertheless, very clearly what Hitler had in mind. People and races are by nature species-specifically limited, and they may not mix with one another without incurring the punishment of decay and finally extinction. The rest of the chapter clarifies his ideas even further by way of examples. Hitler subdivides mankind into three categories: founders of culture, bearers of culture, and destroyers of culture. [14] Only the Aryans are founders of culture ("the Greek spirit plus Germanic technology"), an example of culture-bearers would be the Japanese, while the Jews are destroyers of culture. The entire rest of the chapter is devoted to the last of the three categories.

Four years later Hitler stated his theory of race and history once more, on the first pages of his *Secret Book.* He did not give up the postulate of racial purity, but this time, significantly, he did not repeat his absurd analogy between the animal kingdom and the realm of man. Instead, he now views as central the struggle between the races. This idea was undoubtedly influenced by the Darwinian expression of the "struggle for existence." [15]

The central concept in all this is that of the instinct for self-preservation. Hitler had already mentioned it repeatedly in *Mein Kampf,* [16] but he had not yet given it its appropriate place in his racial theory. Thus we read earlier only that "In the end it is always the drive for self-preservation which wins out." [17] Or: "The instinct of preserving the species is the first cause of the formation of human communities." [18] These statements had then been applied to various realms, among them that of marriage, whose sole meaning and purpose had been seen as the "propagation and preservation of the species and the race." [19] But in *Mein Kampf* the concept of self-preservation had never been more than a borrowed cliché.

In the *Secret Book,* however, this concept acquired greater specificity and became the necessary cause of the struggle for life in the context of Hitler's theory of history. [20] This time Hitler even went about it in a fairly systematic way. He started with the concept of the struggle for existence, "because in truth that struggle for daily bread, both in peace and in war, is an eternal battle against thousands upon thousands of obstacles just as life itself is an eternal struggle against death. For men know as little why they live as does any other creature of the world. Only life is filled with the longing to preserve itself." To this very fundamental longing correspond "the two powerful life-instincts, hunger and love." That had already been stated in *Mein Kampf,* where Hitler had referred to the struggle between animals as originating "less from reasons of inner aversion than from hunger and love." [21] But there the idea had not been pursued any further. Now, however, it was both generalized and refined: "While the appeasement of eternal hunger guarantees self-preservation, the satisfaction of love assures the continuance of the race. In truth these two drives are the rulers of life." This is equally true for individual animals and animal species as it is for individual human beings and for peoples. "A nation (*Volkskörper*) is only a multitude of more or less similar individual beings." On the one hand, they all want to live, i.e. not to die of hunger, while on the other hand they also want to live on in their offspring, i.e. not to become extinct. They want to self-preserve and to propagate themselves.

For this they need a certain space to live in, a

certain *Lebensraum*. This term, derived from social Darwinism, had also been used repeatedly in the two volumes of *Mein Kampf*;[22] it was used mostly in its original descriptive sense [23] and only rarely in reference to demands in foreign policy. This pattern remains the same in the *Secret Book*. The drives for self-preservation and propagation are seen as unlimited, but the possibilities for their fulfillment are limited because the space within which they can find fulfillment is limited. The "logical consequence" of this is "a struggle in all its forms for the possibility of maintaining this life." Or, put differently, "Countless are the species of all the earth's organisms, unlimited at any moment in all individuals is their instinct for self-preservation as well as their longing for continuance, yet the space in which the whole life process takes place is limited. The struggle for existence and continuance in life waged by billions upon billions of organisms takes place on the surface of an exactly measured sphere. The compulsion to engage in the struggle for existence lies in the limitation of the living space; but in the life-struggle for this living space. lies also the basis for evolution." [24]

The last remark, tacked onto the sentence, expresses another important law of nature into which Hitler does not go in any detail here, perhaps because he had mentioned it again and again in *Mein Kampf*. It is the "basically aristocratic principle of nature" of the victory of the stronger over the weaker as a means "to breed life as a whole towards a higher level" and as the "precondition for all human progress." [25] What nature wants everywhere "is the victory of the stronger and the annihilation or unconditional surrender of the weaker." [26] This "iron law of necessity and of the right of the victory of the best and the strongest" [27] is, of course, equally operative in history where it corresponds "to the innermost will of nature, as nature restores that free play of forces which is bound to lead to a permanent mutual higher breeding, until finally the best of mankind, having acquired the possession of this earth, are given a free road for their activity in domains which will lie partly above, partly outside it." [28] World domination thus appears, with a certain amount of consistency, as the distant final goal of history. "We all sense that in the distant future problems could approach man for conquest of which only a higher race, as the master nation, based upon the means and the possibilities of an entire globe, will be called upon." [29] Based on this theoretical outlook, Hitler said in 1930: "Every being strives for expansion and every nation strives for world domination." [30]

Hitler asserts that culture came into being only by the subjugation of the weak, and he paints the following picture of cultural development: "Aryan tribes (often with a really ridiculously small number of their people) subjugate foreign peoples, and now, stimulated by the special living conditions of the new territory (fertility, climatic conditions, etc.) and favored by the size of the labor force in the shape of people of an inferior kind now at their disposal, they develop the mental and organizational abilities which have slumbered within them. Often, in the course of a few millennia or even centuries they create cultures which initially bear completely the inner features of their character, adapted to the already mentioned special qualities of the soil as well as to those of the subjected people. Finally, however, the conquerors deviate from the purity of their blood which they originally maintained, they begin to mix with the subjected natives, and thus end their own existence; for the fall of man in Paradise has always been followed by expulsion from it." [31]

From all of this Hitler derived his fundamental principle of history. Since space is limited, but the two instincts of peoples for preservation are unlimited, it follows that nations have to wage eternal war for space; and, inasmuch as this is the essential reality of their existence, history becomes the life struggle of nations for living space.

If this then is the meaning of history and if politics is nothing but history in the making, then the goal of politics follows with absolute necessity, "then politics is in truth the execution of a nation's struggle for existence." [32] Since this is in turn the highest, indeed the only, goal of politics, all the distinctions between war and peace on the one hand and between foreign and domestic policies on the other lose their traditional significance. All of them, each in its own way, become completely subservient to the sole goal of all politics and thus of the meaning of history.

By its very definition the struggle for life is, of course, linked with the use of force. If one keeps this clearly in mind, "the two concepts − a policy of peace or war − immediately sink into nothingness." That does not mean incessant war. "A policy which is fundamentally bellicose," which "leads to the slow bleeding away of the best, most valuable elements of a nation," will be "precisely as harmful and devastating in its effects" as "a policy which is fundamentally peaceful" and which, consequently, leads to emigration, to birth control, and thus "to a lowering of the value of a people altogether." Instead, politics must "always choose the weapons of its struggles so that life in the highest sense of the word is served. For one does not make politics in order to be able to die, rather one may at times call upon men to die so that a nation may live." [33] Looked at in this way, "even wars lose their isolated character of more or less immense surprises; they become integrated instead into a natural, indeed self-evident, system of a fundamental, well-grounded, permanent development of a people." [34]

94

Thus war becomes a virtually normal condition, and it is a secondary question of expediency whether one uses weapons or other means to wage it.

This also eliminates the traditional differentiation between foreign and domestic politics. Hitler summarized his deliberation as follows: "If the task of politics is the execution of a people's struggle for existence, and if the struggle for existence of a people, in the last analysis, consists of safeguarding the necessary amount of space for nourishing a specific population, and if this whole process is a question of the employment of a people's strength, the following concluding definitions result therefrom:

Politics is the art of carrying out a people's struggle for its earthly existence.

Foreign policy is the art of safeguarding the momentary, necessary living space, in quantity and quality, for a people.

Domestic policy is the art of preserving the necessary employment of force for this in the form of its race value and numbers." [35]

Thus domestic policy is merely a function of foreign policy, which incidentally explains the primacy of the latter in Hitler's thought; but it has some special tasks nevertheless. It has to provide the means of power for the life struggle in the shape of the value and the numbers of the people. This introduces two more important concepts. The one referring to numbers is so self-evident that Hitler did not think it necessary to explain it in any detail. It contains the whole complex of problems known as population policies. A people can, of course, secure the living space necessary at any given time only if it has a sufficient number of soldiers to either defend or conquer it and if it has a sufficient number of farmers to cultivate it. If, for example, in order to make do with its available living space, a people limits its birth rate — which it should not do if it wants to preserve the value of its population [36] — then it leaves itself open to the danger of falling prey, sooner or later, to a people which grows faster and is stronger. It will be annihilated. But if it encourages an increase in population — which it must do for other reasons as well — then its living space will sooner or later become too limited and it has to proceed to an expansion of its living space which, as a rule, means war. This can be called Hitler's dialectics of history: increasing population means insufficient living space and leads to war for new living space; decreasing or static population figures mean that others become stronger, which also leads to war in which the weaker nation will, moreover, lose the living space it had before. History is an incessant and merciless struggle for life. "Therefore, he who wants to live must fight and he who does not want to fight in this world of eternal struggle, does not deserve to be alive." [37]

But population numbers alone are not sufficient. One has to add to them racial value *(Rassenwert),* also referred to as value of a people *(Volkswert)* or value of blood *(Blutswert).* Once again, Hitler paid little attention to terminological precision. Not only are the terms used interchangeably, the value of a people is also, on the one hand, "the truly eternal factor for the greatness and importance of a people" while it simultaneously contains, on the other hand, two subcategories: namely, that of the personality value of a people as well as that of its drive for self-preservation — which, incidentally, is not necessarily identical with the synonymous instinct of all living beings mentioned above. Thus the value of a people, it should be noted, is simultaneously used as a category in its own right and as a subset thereof. As a category it is subdivided into the value of a people as such, into the personality value, and into the drive for self-preservation. [38] Such conceptual distinctions should perhaps not be overemphasized for, once again, the matter itself is clear enough. In *Mein Kampf*, all of these concepts had been adumbrated and, as it were, pre-formed, [39] but they had been described primarily *ex negativo*, as will be shown shortly. It is only in the *Secret Book* that they are defined in positive terms and that they are given their place in the broad context of the *Weltanschauung*.

The value of a people is the most important factor, "for the source of a people's whole power does not lie in its possession of weapons or in the organization of its army, but in its inner value," [40] i.e. its value as a people *(Volkswert)*. Every people differs from all others, every race from all others, just as all human beings differ from each other. There are people of a higher and those of a lower race, stronger and weaker people, better and worse ones. In short, "every people, apart from the numerical value deriving from its count, also has a specific value which is peculiar to it." This value is given in nature; it is, however, largely a product of the will and of con-sciousness — in an astonishing contrast to Hitler's other-wise deterministic racial theory. "The importance of the blood value of a people, however, only becomes totally effective when this value is recognized by a people, properly valued and appreciated. Peoples who do not understand this value or who no longer have a feeling for it for lack of a natural instinct, thereby immediately also begin to lose it. Blood mixing and lowering of the race are then the consequences which, to be sure, at the beginning are not seldom introduced through a so-called predilection for things foreign, which in reality is an underestimation of one's own cultural values as against those of alien peoples. . . . For this reason international-mindedness is to be regarded as the mortal enemy of these values."

Since all men are not the same, it follows that the

personality value is not the same "among all the members within a people."[41] Consequently majorities — which are based, after all, on the assumption that all men are equal — have never "wrought creative achievements. Never have they given discoveries to mankind. The individual person has always been the originator of human progress." Thus a people which either has or wants to have racial value must and will recognize personality value and will therefore appropriately free itself from egalitarian or majority constructs. "Once a people installs the majority as the rulers of its life, that is to say, once it introduces present-day democracy in the Western conception, it will not only damage the importance of the concept of personality, but block the effectiveness of the personality value. Through a formal construction of its life it prevents the rise and the work of individual creative persons." It eliminates the possibility "for the rise of a vigorous leadership," and thus "one of the most powerful sources of a people's strength is blocked."

"The third factor of the strength of a people is its healthy, natural instinct for self-preservation. From it result numerous heroic virtues, which by themselves make a people take up the struggle for life. No state leadership will be able to have great successes, if the people whose interests it must represent is too cowardly and wretched to stake itself for these interests. No state leadership, of course, can expect that a people possess heroism, which it itself does not educate to heroism. Just as internationalism harms and thereby weakens the existing race value, and as democracy destroys the personality value, so pacifism paralyzes the natural strength of the self-preservation of peoples."[42]

These three factors, the value of a people, the personality value, and the drive for self-preservation — or, as one might call them, nationalism, the Führer principle, and heroism or militarism — are of the utmost importance for Hitler's *Weltanschauung.* As mentioned above, they had all been foreshadowed in *Mein Kampf* but essentially in terms of their opposites, internationalism, democracy, and pacifism; and they had not yet been combined into a trinity under the general heading of racial value. This combination occurred for the first time, to the best of our knowledge, in a speech given at Nuremberg on July 21, 1927, in which Hitler said: "Then things will come to that state which great parties proclaim in their programs, namely to a people which is internationally oriented, which is ruled according to the program of democracy, and which rejects struggle and preaches pacifism. A people has lost its inner value as soon as it has incorporated into itself these three vices of mankind, as it has eliminated its racial value, preached internationalism, given up its self-direction and has put in its place majority rule, i.e. incompetence, and has begun to indulge in the brotherhood of mankind." [43] These ideas were then fully developed in his *Secret Book* and were incorporated into the context of a theory of history. After that they gained such significance that Hitler repeated them in full detail, for example, in his well-known speech to industrialists from Western Germany delivered at Düsseldorf on January 27, 1932. [44]

The absolutely crucial importance of Hitler's idea of the above three factors in the total context of his *Weltanschauung* lies in the fact that the originators and bearers of all three counterpositions are the Jews. In itself, this discovery was nothing new. But by incorporating it into his theory of history, Hitler established for the first time a logical link between his foreign policy conception and his antisemitism. They were synthesized in his view of history. With this, Hitler's *Weltanschauung* had finally achieved the kind of consistency for which he had groped such a long time. Now the points of his program had found a meaningful *locus* in a broader system from which they, in turn, could be logically deduced.

The fact that the Jews were the carriers of internationalism, democracy, and pacifism still belonged, as it were, to Hitler's old antisemitic armory. It did not, originally, derive from any theory but rather from his observations of everyday political events, and it served a polemical purpose. I have already referred above to Hitler's charge of Jewish internationalism, levelled untiringly since 1920. [45] In almost every speech, as well as in well-nigh every chapter of *Mein Kampf,* the substantiating passages for this charge are so incredibly numerous that one could fill many pages by merely enumerating them. It was by far the most significant charge raised in Hitler's antisemitism. "Jewish" and "international" became virtually identical, so much so that Hitler, from the beginning of the twenties to his death, rarely used one of these terms without the other. This appellation had far-reaching implications for him. It was for this reason that the Jews became the instigators of all international programs, such as Marxism, Socialism, universal peace, the League of Nations, Freemasonry, and so on. Thus when Hitler spoke of Marxism as being Jewish, he referred not only to the Jew Karl Marx but also, beyond that, to the international character of Marxism. [46] In this sense, the German Social Democratic Party also was Jewish for Hitler, *a priori* and *per definitionem,* quite regardless of whether its leading proponents were Jews or not, because the Social Democrats propounded the idea of the international solidarity of the workers. [47]

The Jews were, however, not only international and internationalistic but also egalitarian — which constitutes Hitler's second charge against them. To him, the idea of the equality of all men was Jewish. [48] It repudiated the "aristocratic principle of nature," but the Jews attempted "to play a trick on nature," saying — brazenly and stupidly — that "Man conquers Nature!" [49] And thus they put "in the place of the eternal privilege of force and strength, the mass of numbers and their dead weight." [50] Their final goal was, first of all, the victory of democracy and the rule of parliamentarism. "It corresponds most closely to their requirements because it eliminates the personality — and in its place puts the majority of stupidity, incompetence, and last, but not least, cowardice." [51] Second, and ultimately, the Jews began "to replace the idea of democracy by that of the dictatorship of the masses" [52] — which links this particular charge with the earlier one of internationalism and Marxism. And third, and finally, the Jews were pacifistic. Only they had an interest in "the general pacifistic paralyzation of the national instinct for self-preservation," "the progressing pacifist Marxist paralyzation of our body politic." [53]

Thus the three charges of internationalism, egalitarianism, and pacifism had already been raised in *Mein Kampf*, although in scattered form and mixed with others. Equally prefigured was the reasoning concerning the special position of the Jews. Hitler emphasized repeatedly and with some force that they did not constitute a religious community, nor were they nomads. [54] Instead, he always referred to them as a people or race, [55] and they were thus not distinguished from other peoples or races. Like the others, the Jews also placed great emphasis on the "purity of [their] blood." [56] There was only one thing which differentiated them from all others: they were a people without a territory, without a state with specific territorial boundaries; or, more accurately, their state was completely unlimited territorially. "The Jewish State was never spatially limited in itself; it was universally unlimited in respect to space, but it was restricted to the collectivity of a race. This is the reason why this people always forms a State

101

within other States." [57] This was neither an accident, nor was it the result of historical development. It was totally irrelevant to Hitler that once there had been a Jewish territorial state. To him the real cause was found in the lack of racial value of the Jews. "Therefore also the Jewish 'State' (which is supposed to be the living organism for the preservation and the propagation of the race) is territorially completely unlimited. For a certain limitation of a State, formation by space always presupposes an idealistic attitude by the State race, especially and above all a correct conception of the notion 'work.' To the same extent as this attitude is lacking or absent, every attempt at a formation or even at the preservation of a territorially limited State fails. With this, the basis on which alone a culture can be founded is also eliminated." [58]

As noted above, all of this had already been prefigured in the first volume of *Mein Kampf* in 1924. But at that time the grand design of foreign policy and, above all, the theory of history had not yet been fully developed. Thus antisemitic charges and territorial ideas had at first existed side by side, more or less unrelated. They had originated from different sources and were aiming in different directions: towards the elimination of the Jews on the one hand, and towards an expansion of the nation on the other. Here and there some interconnections had, of course, become visible, but they did not indicate anything beyond an attempt at a synthesis. It was only in Hitler's view of history that the synthesis was finally found or rather completed and consummated. Only in 1928, at the end of the *Secret Book,* did Hitler set the keystone of his *Weltanschauung.* [59]

He did so with some hesitation, perhaps because he believed he had already stated everything. He began by saying that he did not regard it as his task at this point "to enter into a discussion of the Jewish question as such." Indeed, all he had to do was to put it into proper perspective and to summarize a few arguments. Jewry, he recapitulated, is a people; a people, of course, which "has special intrinsic characteristics which separate it from all other peoples living on the globe." It is worth noting Hitler's objective and unpolemical tone at this point. Jewry, he continued, is not a religious community and has never had a territorially bounded state; this was "connected with the character of the Jewish people which is lacking in the productive forces for the construction and preservation of its own territorial state." All of this was repetition, but the next idea departed somewhat from those stated before. "Just as every people as a basic tendency of all its earthly actions possesses a mania for self-preservation as its driving force, likewise is it exactly so with Jewry, too." Never before had Hitler gone quite that far in his equation of the Jews with other peoples.

But what, then, was the difference? Was it only the absence of a territorial state? No, the difference was found in the struggle for life: "Only here, in accord with their basically different dispositions, the struggle for existence of Aryan peoples and Jewry is also different in its forms." Now Hitler was able to fit his theory of history into his considerations on the Jewish question. The starting point for the former and its most important principle read (and it was repeated at this point): "The foundation of the Aryan struggle for life is in the soil"; in other words, history is the peoples' life struggle for living space. In this – and Hitler states it almost with regret – the Jewish people cannot participate since it has no territory which it could either preserve or increase. It thus obscures the clear battle lines of history, it runs counter, as it were, to the basic idea of nature, it throws out of joint the world as it should be and as it actually is in every other respect.

103

From this Hitler derives, of necessity, the special unnatural and ahistorical forms of the Jewish struggle for life; for the Jews, like all the others, want to preserve their life and fight for it, of course. But they do so, necessarily, in their own way: "Because of the lack of any productive capacity of its own, the Jewish people cannot carry out the construction of a state, viewed in a territorial sense, but as a support of its own existence it needs the work and creative activities of other nations. Thus, the existence of the Jew himself becomes a parasitical one within the lives of other peoples." Never before had Hitler been able to deduce with such cogency his previously overwhelmingly polemical and propagandistic adjectives drawn from the realm of parasitology. If the soil was "the general basis for an economy" which satisfied "its own needs ... through the productive forces of its own people," and if the Jews neither had nor could have any soil of their own, then they had to live on the "productive forces" of their host nations, then they were parasites.

From these forms of the Jewish struggle for life derived its goals and means. "The ultimate goal of the Jewish struggle for existence is the enslavement of productively active peoples." Even in this the Jews did not differ from anyone else. For according to the intention of nature, the struggle for life meant, after all, the victory of the stronger and the annihilation of the weaker or his unconditional surrender. It was just that the Jew did this too in his own way: "His ultimate goal is the denationalization, the promiscuous bastardization of other peoples, the lowering of the racial level of the highest peoples as well as the domination of this racial mishmash through the extirpation of the folkish intelligentsia and its replacement by the members of its own people." Quite naturally, the objective and the enemy of the Jewish struggle for life were, therefore, not the soil nor – as it would have been in any normal, nature-intended struggle for existence – one or more nations, like the German nation for example, which were to be subjugated and robbed of their soil. The Jews could not do anything like that. Instead, their goal was the denationalization of the world as a whole. The objective and the enemy of their struggle for existence was all nations, was the principle of nation as such, the principle of nature, the principle of history; was – as Hitler had put it on an earlier occasion – "the work of the Lord". [60] The fight against the Jews was therefore not a national task; it was a task for all mankind, and it had to assume the universalist-missionary characteristics already noted above.

The means and weapons employed by the Jew in this struggle were all those which "are in keeping with the whole complex of his character." They could be subdivided into several categories. "Therefore in domestic politics within the individual nations he fights first for equal rights and later for superrights." This was the charge of egalitarianism. Because of his lack of a territorial state, the Jew was lower, unlike other peoples; and it was for this reason that he asserted, against nature, that all men are equal, including himself. Only by this could he establish for his struggle for existence a basis which promised success. One had to see through the fact that these were "as much strategems in his war of survival as those of other peoples in armed combat." Since the Jew could not fight with the sword, he had to spread the poison of pacifism. Once this point of departure had been reached, the Jew continued to fight on an international level. "In foreign policy he tries to bring nations into a state of unrest, to divert them from their true interests, and to plunge them into reciprocal wars and in this way gradually to rise to mastery over them with the help of the power of money and propaganda."

This sentence contains the charge of internationalism. International ideas, however, link peoples to each other instead of separating them. It may still come to wars, but they no longer reflect the true interests of the peoples, namely the fight for living space. Thus Jewish internationalism obstructs the struggle for existence as it is intended by nature, and destroys the meaning of history.

With this synthesis of all of his earlier notions (of which he, significantly, did not give up any part in any way essential), Hitler had achieved a view of history and he had constructed from it a *Weltanschauung* from which he could then proceed to deduce logically all of his political demands. It is on this basis that the programmatic thinker Hitler confirms and defines for the politician Hitler the dual, yet also unified, task of his life. He had to annihilate the Jews, thus restoring the meaning of history, and within the thus restored, nature-intended struggle for existence, he at the same time had to conquer new living space for the German people. Each of these tasks was inextricably linked to the other; indeed, they were the mutually necessary preconditions for each other. Unless the Jews were annihilated there would very soon no longer be any struggle for living space, nor therefore any culture, and consequently nations would die out; not just the German nation, but ultimately all nations. But if, on the other hand, the German people failed to conquer new living space, it would die out because of that and the Jews would triumph.

Insofar as other people still possessed racial value and had not yet been weakened by Jewish internationalism, they too fought for living space. To that extent and as a consequence of this they were the natural rivals of the German people, which also had to be able to win its fight for new living space. It therefore had to and could

ally itself with those other nations which retained sufficient racial value for expansion[61] but which wanted to
do so in areas of the world in which Germany did not
intend to expand. Such a nation was Italy with its
expansionist tendencies in the Mediterranean and in
Africa, and such a nation was Great Britain with its
overseas expansionism, although in the latter case one
had to make qualifications because of the already far
advanced state of Jewish influence there. For its part,
Germany would first get rid of the obstacle of France
and would then expand at the expense of Russia. There
the Jew had already been completely victorious. This
fact would, on the one hand, make war easier since the
Jew had, after all, no racial value capable of forming a
territorial state; on the other hand, it would impart to
the war a universalist-missionary character precisely because of the rule of the Jews in Russia. By destroying
the Jews there, the Russian state would be weakened
and thus the conquest of new living space for Germany
would be rendered easier. By conquering this living
space, international Jewry, which together with Bolshe-
vism had recently established its world headquarters in
Russia, would be dealt a decisive defeat.

Thus everything fitted together. There is no need to
point out to any civilized human being that this *Weltanschauung,* whose means were exclusively war and murder, openly acknowledged from the very beginning, has
never been surpassed by any other in primitivity and
brutality. But that makes it no less of a self-consistent
synthesis.

CHAPTER VI

From the Ordinary
to the Extraordinary

THE genesis of Hitler's *Weltanschauung* did not, of course, proceed along the lines of thought just described above. It is highly improbable that any world view was ever derived from previously discovered general principles; Hitler's certainly was not. That can be readily shown from the sources. Hitler's antisemitism, for example, was thus not the deductive result of his view of history but had originated many years earlier. Similarly, the plan of a war of conquest had been decided upon long before it ever received its theoretical justification in terms of Hitler's system of thought. More important still is the fact that the two core elements of the *Weltanschauung* had been fully developed before their logical correlation and mutual interdependence were established. I have therefore deliberately used the term "synthesis," i.e. an ex post facto systematization, which did not bring anything new in its details but simply pulled together into an ordered coherence all the notions which already existed previously.

How then did Hitler's *Weltanschauung* develop? He himself has provided an answer to this question. The autobiographical organization of *Mein Kampf* had, among other things, precisely the purpose, as we are told in the preface to the first volume, to "describe my own development." According to this source, "my first ideals were formed" during early childhood.[1] He became a nationalist in secondary school *(Realschule)* and "learned to understand the meaning of history." [2] But his real schooling for life took place in Vienna, where he spent the years between 1907 and 1913, i.e. the years between his eighteenth and his twenty-fourth birthdays. It was then that his "eyes were opened" to the twin dangers of Marxism and Jewry which threatened the existence of the German people. He learned as he had "never done before" and was thus able to write later: "At that time I formed an image of the world and a *Weltanschauung* which became the granite foundation for my actions. I have had to add but little to that which I learned then and I have had to change nothing." [3] During the years 1909 and 1910 he studied "practically anything" concerning social problems on which he could get books. [4] A short time later he encountered Social Democracy: "My opinion about it was enlarged and deepened in the course of the years, but I had no reason to change it." [5] The events within the Austrian monarchy, "which are the constant causes of the decline of nations and States and which possess significance for our era as well," also helped — as he wrote in 1924 — "to establish the principles of my political thought." [6] Thus Vienna "was and remained for me the hardest, but also the most thorough, school of my life. . . . In that city I received the basis of a *Weltanschauung* in general and a political way of looking at things in particular which later on I had only to supplement in individual instances, but which never again deserted me." [7]

"In the spring of 1912," the autobiography continues, "I came to Munich for good." What attracted young Hitler most about Germany "apart from my professional work . . . was again the study of current political events, among them especially those concerning foreign politics." [8] In this chapter (IV), as has already been shown above, [9] Hitler provided the first exposition of his territorial plans, and he intimated, although he never said so explicitly, that he had developed these ideas during that time in Munich. His plans are, in fact, based on an analysis and critique of German prewar policies. He also studied at the time Bismarck's anti-Socialist legislation and concluded the chapter with the already familiar phrase: "Gradually I gained a truly granite foundation for my own convictions, so that from that time on I was never forced to make any changes in my inner attitudes towards this question." [10] He went even further: "In the years 1913 and 1914, I initially expressed in various circles (some of which today stand faithfully by the movement) the conviction that the question of the future of the German nation is the question of the destruction of Marxism. In the fatal German policy of alliances I saw only one of the after-effects caused by the destructive working of this doctrine."[11]

Hitler describes his experiences during the First World War in a similar fashion: "There were two things in those days which, deep down, angered me and which I considered detrimental." [12] They were on the one hand Germany's propaganda policy, and on the other hand the fact that Jews were not being ruthlessly extermi-nated in those days. [13] "I talked openly about this to my more intimate friends. What is more, I now conceived for the first time the idea of becoming active in politics later on." [14] This must have occurred at the beginning of the war; a few pages later, we read about the year 1915: "During those months, I fully felt, for the first time, the whims of fortune which kept me at the front in a place where any chance move on the part of a Negro could gun me down, while I could have rendered a different service to my country in some other place. For I was bold enough to believe even then that I would be suc-cessful in this." [15] It is well known that the final decision "to become a politician" was reached in November 1918 in a hospital in Pasewalk. [16]

This decision was translated into action by Hitler's joining the German Workers' Party in September, 1919. At that time, sent out by his commanding officer for surveillance of a meeting of that party, Hitler received from the founder of the party, Anton Drexler, a copy of his brochure called "My Political Awakening." He read "the entire little document with interest; for in it an experience was reflected which I had personally gone through in a similar fashion twelve years earlier." [17] Twelve years before 1919 means 1907, and thus the beginning of his time in Vienna. In 1919 Hitler was thirty years old, which was precisely the right time, for Hitler held the conviction – as he wrote – that "a man should not take any active public part in politics before the age of thirty, except in cases of outstanding ability. He should not do so because up to that time the formation of a general platform takes place from which he examines the various political problems and defines his own final attitude towards them. The man who has now matured at least mentally may or should take part in the political guidance of the community only after reaching a fundamental *Weltanschauung* and, with it, a stability of his own way of looking at individual current problems." [18]

This description of a seemingly very straight and logical intellectual development deserves our most active disbelief. Years ago, historical inquiry into Hitler's youth has shown that in many details the autobiographical passages of *Mein Kampf* project an extremely approximate and in many cases simply erroneous image of the external circumstances of the years of Hitler's youth. [19] The present study of Hitler's *Weltanschauung* merely underscores this impression where his internal development is concerned; it is, however, not easy to contradict

Hitler's assertions that he had first developed one or the other of his ideas at one or another point in time. A considerable number of deviations from historical truth are nevertheless perfectly clear even in such cases. Thus we have seen that Hitler's conception of foreign policy underwent a fundamental transformation, which can be documented in detail, from ordinary revisionism to his imperialism of living space between 1919 and 1924 and even beyond. It is also undoubtedly false, and improbable to boot, when Hitler insists that he had developed this conception before 1914. He is also in error with his statement that he had come to Munich in the spring of 1912, especially when he adds "for good," as if he had ever been there before. In reality, he moved there in the spring of 1913 and it was for the first time. There is also no supporting evidence in his numerous antisemitic speeches between 1919 and 1924, in which, as we know, he did demand the expulsion of the Jews, for his claim that he had conceived of his bloody and radical solution to the Jewish question as early as 1914 or 1915. Indeed, the ultimate completion of his *Weltanschauung* took place only after the writing of the autobiography, several attempts to predate it to Hitler's time in Vienna notwithstanding.

Apart from all these details, there remains the alleged consistency of development – which, by the standards of human experience, must raise some doubts. Here we have a young man. He has hardly grown up when, after some initial and basic reading in history, he begins at age eighteen to lay the cornerstones of his *Weltanschauung* in systematic fashion one after the other. He never has to change a thing, he finally completes it after twelve years, and he does so precisely in his thirtieth year at the age of maturity required by his theory. That does not seem to be the kind of story written by life. Hitler's attempt at conscious stylization is only too transparent.

In fact, Hitler himself acknowledged as much and justified it. Why should a man not become active publicly in politics before he has reached thirty? The answer to this question reads like an explanation of his stylized autobiography. A man should not do it because otherwise he will run the danger "that some day he will have to change his attitude towards vital questions, or, despite his better knowledge and belief, will have to uphold points of view which reason and conviction have long since rejected. The first case is very embarrassing for him, for now personally uncertain, he has no longer the right to expect that his followers have the same unshakable belief in him as before; such a reversal on the part of the leader brings uncertainty to his followers and frequently a certain feeling of embarrassment vis-à-vis those whom they have been fighting. But in the second case there may happen what we so frequently see today: to the same extent to which the leader no longer believes in what he says, his defense will become hollow and shallow . . . until he finally sacrifices what is left of the leader in order to end up as a 'politician,' which means as a kind of man whose only real conviction is to have no convictions." [20]

This passage — which, incidentally, makes an almost imperceptible transition from "man in general" to the "leader" — is very significant. It shows Hitler's almost panic fear of changing one's mind. A leader who does so has not improved himself, he has changed sides and has discredited himself. He is in honor bound then "to face the ultimate consequences." "In such a case he must for all future times renounce at least all public political activity. As he has already been the victim of a fundamental error of judgement once, there is the possibility that it will happen again." [21] In other words, the leader has to be infallible. If he is that, then "his learning will no longer be a relearning of principles but an adding to what he has learned." This will please his followers; "the visible organic growth of the leader will give them satisfaction." [22]

It was apparently this kind of satisfaction which Hitler intended to give to the readers of *Mein Kampf.* Never, he emphasized again and again, did he relearn; never did he have to change anything. He always merely added to his knowledge, expanded or deepened his views. This description did not necessarily have to correspond to reality; but it made good sense politically, and it turned, almost naturally, into a stylistic tool with a political purpose. Even if Hitler had not himself furnished the theoretical explanation, one would have been led to suspect that even an autobiography could, of course, be no mere end in itself. Like everything else from the Party Program all the way to the State, it was a means to an end, wholly subservient to political goals.

When read in this way, the autobiography reveals the structure of an "organic development" which is astonishing indeed. In his first chapter, Hitler "at the age of fifteen . . . already understood the difference between dynastic 'patriotism' and popular 'nationalism.' " [23] The second chapter was devoted to the social question and provided what, on the basis of the first chapter, was of course a national Socialism. The insight into the counter-forces simultaneously brought with it the switch to antisemitism. Thus the foundations for an antisemitic National Socialism had been laid. Further political considerations from the time in Vienna led, in the third chapter, to the problems of domestic policy, especially the problem of parliamentarism, and to the German question concerning the relationship between Austria and Germany. The fourth chapter then brought, as an organic result of the move to Munich, an occupation with foreign policy. The First World War served as a teacher of the methods of political skills; in Chapter V concerning the fight against the Jews and in Chapter VI in the field of propaganda. This completed the years of learning, and in his seventh chapter Hitler was now ready to decide upon becoming a politician. Chapter VIII is, quite consistently, entitled "The Beginning of my Political Career," and in Chapter XI he joins the Party. "It was the most momentous decision of my life. There could not, and must not be, any turning back from it." [24] Thus the "organic growth of the leader" and, consequently, the autobiographical part of *Mein Kampf* had come to an end. From now on the life of the Führer no longer yielded any further instructive satisfaction. There was nothing else to learn from it because the Führer had learned everything there was to learn and thus the autobiography receded into the background. Memoirs were not intended. There were two more general chapters, the tenth on "The Causes of the Collapse" and the eleventh on "Nation and Race." The twelfth and final chapter already prepared the transition to Volume Two; "The movement took its course." [25] This second volume, as we already mentioned, was organized along lines quite analogous to the first by following closely the development of the Party.

All of this makes it virtually impossible to maintain the widely held view that *Mein Kampf* is "a sequential arrangement of chapters which are complete in themselves but lack any continuous structure." [26] A careful reading reveals instead that the opposite is true. Hitler often shows little auctorial discipline within the chapters themselves and digresses into other questions. But he always returns to his topic, at times with almost forced transitions, and above all, he adheres carefully to the apparently planned sequence of the chapters. By mentioning the questions to be dealt with at the start, he often practically announces the organization of the book, just as he repeats the dominant ideas at the end of a discussion. Handwritten drafts of some of his early speeches have survived, which contain their outline in abbreviated form. [27] There is a considerable probability that such outlines also existed for *Mein Kampf;* indeed, the attempt to reconstruct them from the text is by no means hopeless. It is true that Hitler was not very systematic either as a thinker or as a writer, but an interpretation of his writings and speeches does not pose any special difficulties; if one reads them carefully and repeatedly, the interpretation makes their organizational principles readily apparent.

Mein Kampf does, however, reflect the development of Hitler's *Weltanschauung* only in stylized form and hence, to a large extent, as deliberate falsification. It was neither derived by deduction from previously discovered general principles, nor did it follow the kind of inductive method the autobiography is trying to suggest. [28] The present inquiry proceeded, therefore, from the premise that all sources were to be accepted as having information value only for the period during which they originated, and that Hitler's autobiographical remarks were not to be accepted as true unless proven to be correct. In accordance with this method, the first volume of *Mein Kampf,* for instance, was used as a source only for the year 1924, i.e. the time it was written; not, however, for Hitler's alleged development from his early childhood onward. This methodological circumspection seems to have been entirely correct and appropriate. The protracted analysis of the autobiography was nevertheless useful. While it has indeed shown the unreliability of the autobiography as a historical source, it has also provided many valuable insights and a better understanding of

Hitler which, in turn, permit us to pose anew the question of the development of his *Weltanschauung.*

This study has to begin essentially with the year 1919 since, apart from a few exceptions, there are almost no contemporary sources extant for the time before that date and the later sources are unreliable in principle. Thus the first three decades of Hitler's life recede once again into a mist of uncertainty, i.e. precisely that period during which he himself claims to have fully developed his *Weltanschauung.* Everything unearthed by historical research about this period, as far as his intellectual development and not the external circumstances of his life are concerned, is based almost exclusively on Hitler's own statements and thus rests on a very shaky foundation.

But starting with 1919, the sources begin to flow so copiously that one can paint a more or less distinct, largely datable, and differentiated picture. It is important to remember at the outset that by 1919 the development of Hitler's *Weltanschauung* was by no means completed, despite his assertions to the contrary, but that it actually had only begun. At age thirty, Hitler is a conventional antisemite and a conventional revisionist in matters of foreign policy. Neither of these attitudes was unusual at the time. Hitler was certainly already more radical than many others in his demand that the Jews should be removed altogether, which probably meant their expulsion, and in the warlike nature of his revisionism. But in neither of the two cases did his ideas at that time show the kind originality they were to achieve later.

It is only in the year 1920 that, starting out from these conventional foundations, he begins a process of developing and perfecting his ideas which is to last several years. Now, for the first time, Hitler attacks the

Jews for their so-called internationalism; and, for the first time, he regards Italy as a potential ally for the war of revision against France. It is by no means impossible, in fact it is even probable on the basis of general experience, that certain rudimentary ideas had existed previously. A letter by Hitler, dated February, 1915, provides one of the few clues for this assumption. Letters by Hitler are rare for any period of his life; this one is particularly exceptional. Among Hitler's handwritten letters this is probably the longest and of the early ones in all likelihood the only one containing anything political. For many pages Hitler describes his experiences at the front and closes the letter as follows (the quotation preserves Hitler's writing style): "I am often thinking about Munich and every one of us has only one wish, that it may soon come to a settling of accounts with the rabble, that we'll come to blows, no matter what the price, and that those of us who will be lucky enough to see our native country again will find it purer and freer from foreign influences *(Fremdländerei)*, that by the sacrifices and agonies which now so many hundreds of thousands of us endure every day that by the river of blood which flows here daily against an international world of enemies, not only will Germany's external enemies be smashed, but also our domestic internationalism be broken up. That would be worth more than any territorial gains. In the case of Austria things will happen as I have always said they would." [29]

At least the term "internationalism" makes an early appearance here; it will emerge again only after 1920. But the rest of these lines seems to corroborate our interpretation. They do not permit us to infer a writer who will assert later on that he developed his most important political ideas at that earlier time. Neither here nor in the later letter of 1919 does he as yet link internationalism with the Jews. His remarks appear instead as rather commonplace. Nationalism and a hatred of foreign influences, annexionism plus an unclear but obviously not very flattering prediction about Austria — those are the ingredients of that early world of his ideas. The later Hitler is, no doubt, already recognizable; but it is equally beyond any doubt that this letter does nothing to refute the assumption that the actual development of his *Weltanschauung* began to take shape after World War I.

This development continued apace after 1920. We have traced it in the preceding chapters. At Landsberg, in 1924, the radicalization of his antisemitism took place, as did the transformation of his foreign policy ideas from revisionism to an imperialism of living space. The latter was the most important of all modifications although, from one particular point of view, it too was only an expansion of earlier ideas. The war against France was retained and was merely given a different function. This reveals an important trait in Hitler's development of his *Weltanschauung*.

His panic fear of changing one's mind has already been mentioned. It now becomes apparent that this fear corresponded to an almost equally frantic attempt to combine ideas into a logical synthesis once they were discovered, without, however, giving up a single one of them.

This aspiration seems to explain quite well the gradual development of Hitler's *Weltanschauung*. He started out with conventional notions held by the man in the street; notions which were in the air, as it were, or better yet, which lay in the streets. In a second phase he gave them certain less conventional traits by radicalizing his antisemitism, by looking for allies, and finally by arriving at an expansionism directed towards the East. Taken separately, none of these notions was anything either special or new, although they already displayed a considerable originality especially concerning the grand design of foreign policy. The attempted synthesis, in a third phase, of all the individual suggestions and ideas into a self-consistent view of history was, however, certainly original, even if Hitler had found ready-made all its individual elements, such as instinct for self-preservation, struggle for life, and so forth.

The long process by which he fitted together into a system these bits and pieces acquired haphazardly so that finally — to use his own phrase once more — every one of them "is put into the place where it belongs [in] the general picture of the world" [30] —that was a truly unusual phenomenon which revealed an unusual mind. The genesis of this *Weltanschauung* can be viewed as a slow development from the ordinary to the extraordinary.

This no longer had any direct political significance, for, in principle, the two core elements of the program could also have been translated into practice without being related to each other. But the synthesis may well have provided not only intellectual satisfaction but also a sense of confirmation concerning the appropriateness of the goals. This, in turn, may explain the obstinacy with which Hitler attempted to pursue his political program over the course of twenty years. His self-assurance which knew no doubts, his unswerving and finally self-destructive consistency, may have been derived ultimately from his self-consistent *Weltanschauung*.

Such considerations, however, lead into the realm of speculation and go beyond the purview of my investigation. Its goal was simply an examination and description of Hitler's *Weltanschauung*. Unusual though it was, no one would seriously investigate it had it not been for the fact that this unusual programmatic mind was also an unusual political force. This, or Hitler's politics, could only be mentioned in the present context in the form of occasional digressions. Nor do I contend in any way that his *Weltanschauung* was the cause of Hitler's political impact. It could not be anything of the sort since hardly anyone, and perhaps not even anyone among Hitler's followers and contemporaries, had ever gone to the trouble of trying to understand this *Weltanschauung* in its entirety. But I would contend that such an understanding is of crucial importance for an understanding of Hitler and to that extent also of a significant part of German and European history. It is in this context that the results of this study will have to be tested, and it will have to be judged by the answer to the question whether it contributes anything to a better understanding of that man's policies beyond what we already know. For there is the rub. Everything which has had a historical effect, even though and perhaps precisely because it is repugnant, must be analyzed and understood dispassionately. That is still the primary task of historical scholarship.

Notes

I: The Problem of a National Socialist *Weltanschauung*

1 Adolf Hitler, *Mein Kampf*, 231f. (English translation, 286). The quotations in the German original were all taken from the first edition (Vol. I, 1925; Vol. II, 1927). Since that edition is difficult to obtain, the pagination given here refers to the popular one-volume edition of 1930; almost all later editions have virtually the same pagination, whereas earlier editions number their pages differently. Thus the quotations are taken from the original text, while the reader may readily find the statements and their contexts in the more widely distributed editions. All important later deviations from the original edition are noted in the footnotes. On the question of textual changes, see Hermann Hammer, "Die deutschen Ausgaben von Hitlers *Mein Kampf*," in *Vierteljahrshefte für Zeitgeschichte*, 4 (1956), 161 ff. [Translator's note: The English translations of quotes from *Mein Kampf* are based on the complete and unabridged English edition published by Reynal and Hitchcock, by arrangement with Houghton Mifflin Company, in 1939. Page numbers in parentheses refer to this edition, as above: *Mein Kampf*, 231 (286). The first of these numbers, 231, refers to the German original in the 1930 or later popular editions; the second, 286, refers to the English edition. For the principles guiding minor changes in the use of the English edition, see translator's Foreword.]

2   *Mein Kampf,* 188 (222).

3   Ibid., 21 (30). On the question of the genesis of Hitler's *Weltanschauung* cf. below, Chapter VI of this study.

4   Vol. II, chapters 1 and 5, 409 (563) and 504 (673).

5   Ibid., 506f (675f).

6   Ibid., 422f (581f).

7   Ibid., 420 (579).

8   Ibid., 507 (676).

9   Ibid., 295 (368).

10   Ibid., 229f (284).

11   Ibid., 419 (576).

12   Ibid., 229 (284).

13   Ibid., 295f (368).

14   Ibid., 419 (576).

15   Ibid., 230f (283-285).

16   Ibid., Foreword.

17   Ibid., 232 (286); cf. also Karl Lange, *Hitlers unbeachtete Maximen* (1968).

18   Hermann Rauschning, *Die Revolution des Nihilismus* (1938), 39 and 206; also in a shortened new edition, ed. by Golo Mann (1964), 53 and 147. (English translation, *The Revolution of Nihilism,* 1939.)

19   Ibid., 38 or (in shorter new edition) 52.

20   Ibid., 40 and 37, or 54 and 51.

21   Ibid., 43 or 56.

22   Hermann Rauschning, *Gespräche mit Hitler* (1940), 223 (English translation, *The Voice of Destruction,* Putnam, 1940). It is worth noting that in this book (p. 5) Rauschning asserted once again that *Mein Kampf* did not contain Hitler's real aims, but that it at least permitted a glimpse at his foreign policy goals. In 1938 he had stated that the plans concerning living space in the East as given in *Mein Kampf* were obsolete (op.cit., 352 or 231f.), while they seemed to be in force again by 1940. This example, without detracting from Rauschning's merits, shows that historical scholarship at last should abstain from using his books as if they were primary sources. They never were that, and they are completely redundant today, considering the extant wealth of reliable source material at least for an

understanding of Hitler. A critical study of Rauschning's works would, incidentally, be a worthwhile
research project.

23 This statement is quoted in Georg Lukács, *Die
Zerstörung der Vernunft* (1953), 572; in Helga
Grebing, *Der Nationalsozialismus* (1959), 43; and
in Edith Eucken-Erdsiek, *"Hitler als Ideologe"* in:
Der Führer ins Nichts (1960), 34; not to mention
those authors who accept the gist of this sentence.

24 Harold J. Laski, *Reflections on the Revolution of
Our Time* (1943), 108–110.

25 Alan Bullock, *Hitler: A Study in Tyranny* (1952);
here quoted from the revised English edition of
1962 (Pelican Books), 382 [Translator's note: the
American paperback edition, Harper Torchbooks
(1964), has the same pagination]. This quotation is
used only to indicate an earlier research position. It
is not intended as a criticism, especially since the
author knows from a conversation with Mr. Bullock
that the latter accepts a good deal of the research
results based on sources discovered since he wrote
his study of Hitler. Cf. Bullock's paper on "Hitler
and the Origins of the Second World War" in:
Proceedings of the British Academy, Volume LIII
(1968), 259ff.

26 Bullock, op.cit., 806.

27 Edgar Alexander, *Der Mythus Hitler* (1937), 224ff.

28 Lukács, op.cit., 565ff.

29 Eva G. Reichmann, *Die Flucht in den Hass* (no date
[1956]), 220. (Cf. note 2, Chapter III, below.)

30 This is the subtitle of Martin Broszat, *Der Nationalsozialismus: Weltanschauung, Programm und Wirk-
lichkeit* (1960); (English translation: *German National Socialism: 1919–1945* [1966]).

31 Grebing, op.cit., 43.

32 Eucken-Erdsiek, op.cit., 26 and 41.

33 Broszat, op.cit., 35.

34 Friedrich Glum, *Der Nationalsozialismus* (1962).
Cf. also the frequently similar criticisms of the
books just mentioned in the survey of secondary
literature by Eberhard Kessel, "Zur Geschichte und
Deutung des Nationalsozialismus" in: *Archiv für
Kulturgeschichte,* 45 (1963), 357ff.

35 Glum, op.cit., X.
36 Bullock, *Hitler* (English edition, 1954), 735; this sentence was omitted from the revised English edition of 1962.
37 Walter Görlitz and Herbert A. Quint, *Adolf Hitler* (1952), 627; cf. also Walter Görlitz, *Adolf Hitler* (1960).
38 Helmut Heiber, *Adolf Hitler* (1960), 157.
39 Bullock, *Hitler* (1962), 806.
40 Hans Bernd Gisevius, *Adolf Hitler* (1963), 38.
41 Ibid., 100.
42 Ernst Nolte, *Der Faschismus in seiner Epoche* (1963), 54f. (English translation: *Three Faces of Fascism* [1966], 23). Another attempt at describing Hitler's *Weltanschauung* is that of Klaus Heisig, *Die politischen Grundlagen in Hitlers Schriften, Reden und Gesprächen im Hinblick auf seine Auffassung von Staat und Recht,* Diss.jur. Cologne (1965). Mention should be made that Friedrich Heer, *Der Glaube des Adolf Hitler* (1968), despite its title, contributes almost nothing to the question of Hitler's *Weltanschauung* as posed in this study.
43 *Mein Kampf,* 418f., (575-577).

II: The Outlines of Foreign Policy

1 H.R. Trevor-Roper, *The Last Days of Hitler* (1947), revised edition 1962.
2 H.R. Trevor-Roper, "The Mind of Adolf Hitler," introduction to: *Hitler's Table Talk,* ed. by Trevor-Roper (1953); also H.R. Trevor-Roper, "Hitlers Kriegsziele," in: *Vierteljahrshefte für Zeitgeschichte* 8 (1960), 121ff. (Paper delivered on November 24, 1959). The author wants to thank Mr. Trevor-Roper at this point for a most helpful conversation.
3 H.R. Trevor-Roper, "Kriegsziele," op.cit., 122.
4 H.R. Trevor-Roper, *The Mind,* op.cit., xvii and xxxv.
5 Trevor-Roper referred explicitly to Hitler's distinction between the programmatic thinker and the politician, ibid., xvi.

Notes

6 H.R. Trevor-Roper, "Kriegsziele," op.cit., 133.

7 See especially Günter Schubert, *Anfänge national-
sozialistischer Aussenpolitik* (1963), as well as Fritz
Dickmann, "Machtwille und Ideologie in Hitlers
aussenpolitischen Zielsetzungen vor 1933," in:
Festschrift für Max Braubach (1964), 915ff. The
rest of this chapter is largely based on the introduction of the author's book *Frankreich in Hitlers
Europa* (1966).

8 Ernst Deuerlein (ed.), "Hitlers Eintritt in die Politik
und die Reichswehr," in *VfZG* 7 (1959), 207.

9 Reginald H. Phelps (ed.), "Hitler als Parteiredner im
Jahre 1920," in: *VfZG* 11 (1963), 314.

10 Ibid., 305.

11 Heinz Preiss (ed.), *Adolf Hitler in Franken. Reden
aus der Kampfzeit* (1939), 11. See also Walter Werner Pese, "Hitler and Italien 1920–1926," in: *VfZG*
3 (1955), 113ff.

12 Thus on December 4, 1932, he wrote to Colonel
von Reichenau that he had suggested working for
closer ties with Italy "for roughly twelve years
now"; in: *VfZG* 7 (1959), 435. On July 1, 1940, he
told Italy's ambassador Alfieri that he had antici-
pated a *rapprochement* between Italy and Germany
"twenty years ago"; in: *Akten zur deutschen auswärtigen Politik 1918–1945,* Series D, Vol. X
(1963), 68. Both of these examples, of which there
are more, show by the way how remarkably accurate Hitler's dating could be at times.

13 He first mentioned the ideological argument only a
short time before Mussolini's march on Rome, on
August 17, 1922; Pese, op.cit., 116. He said later
that he had first heard about Fascism in 1921;
Hitler's Table Talk, op.cit., 266.

14 The statement must have been made in either late
1922 or in early 1923; here quoted from Schubert,
op.cit., 77. Cf. also Pese, op.cit., 121ff.

15 Phelps, op.cit., 308.

16 Ibid., 290.

17 See, for instance, Hitler's speech of April 17, 1920;
ibid., 297f.

18 Ernst Boepple (ed.), *Adolf Hitlers Reden* (1925),

55f. The date may refer to the Treaty of Paris (September 3, 1783); cf. *Mein Kampf,* 692 (895).

19 Boepple, op.cit., 93f.

20 Since the completion of *Hitler's Weltanschauung,* one such study has been published: Axel Kuhn, *Hitlers aussenpolitisches Programm* (1970). The author is indebted to Dr. Kuhn for help in various ways and for a stimulating exchange of ideas.

21 Adolf Hitler, "Warum musste ein 8.November kommen?," in: *Deutschlands Erneuerung 8* (1924), 199. Cf. on this Wolfgang Horn, "Ein unbekannter Aufsatz Hitlers aus dem Frühjahr 1924," in: *VfZG* 16 (1968), 280ff.

22 Phelps, op.cit., 289.

23 Boepple, op.cit., 66.

24 *Mein Kampf* (cf. Chapter I, fn.1), 1 (3). The metaphor of the sword and the ploughshare, repeatedly used by Hitler, is an inversion of the well-known metaphor for peace from Isaiah 2,4, which had already been transformed into its warlike opposite in Joel 4,10.

25 This and the other quotations in this paragraph are from *Mein Kampf,* 143-153f (168-184).

26 Cf. Gerhard L. Weinberg, introduction to the German edition of *Hitlers Zweites Buch* (1961), 21f. (Translator's note: The English edition of *Hitler's Secret Book,* intr. by Telford Taylor, tr. by Salvator Attanasio, New York [1961], does not contain Weinberg's meticulous introduction and commentary.)

27 For this and the following quotations, see *Mein Kampf,* 689ff. (892-902).

28 The rest of this chapter of *Mein Kampf* will be treated below in a different context; cf. pp. 38, 55ff.

29 1927 had already been given as the publication date; the Epilogue was written in November, 1926.

30 For this and the following quotations, see *Mein Kampf,* 727ff. (934, 939, 946-948).

31 Ibid., 766f. (949, 978).

32 Ibid., 743 (950f., 952). In this exceptional case the quotation is taken from the 1930 edition; in the first edition this sentence, in an otherwise unchang-

Notes

ed context, had read: "The Persian Empire, once so powerful, is now ripe for collapse . . ." (English translation, 952). For the sake of clarity, Hitler later omitted the metaphoric historical analogy.

33 Ibid., 743 (952); the relationship between foreign policy and racial theory will be treated below.

34 *Mein Kampf,* 697 (901).

35 Ibid., 757 (966).

36 Ibid., 755 (964).

37 Ibid., 36 (47f.).

38 Gerhard L. Weinberg (ed.), *Hitlers Zweites Buch. Ein Dokument aus dem Jahre 1928,* Stuttgart (1961), 45. (English translation: *Hitler's Secret Book,* New York [1961], 4.) [Translator's note: The procedure for indicating citations in the German original and in the English translation used for quotations from *Mein Kampf* will also be followed for this book; cf. above, Chapter I, fn. 1, tr. note.]

39 Cf. *Mein Kampf,* 691f. (894f.).

40 *Zweites Buch,* 167f. (149, 151).

41 Hitler tried to explain that with different arguments, already used in *Mein Kampf,* which were derived from his racial theory and which will be treated in the following chapter; cf. below, Chapter III.

42 Cf. Helmut Heiber (ed.), "Der Generalplan Ost," in: *VfZG* 6 (1958), 281ff.; cf. also *VfZG* 8 (1960), 119.

43 *Zweites Buch,* 173 (156).

44 All notes on this part of the chapter are restricted to the briefest of source references and omit deliberately any mention of the overabundant secondary material.

45 Max Domarus (ed.), *Hitler. Reden und Proklamationen 1932 bis 1945,* Volume I (1962), 235f.

46 *Akten zur deutschen auswärtigen Politik 1918–1945,* Series D, Vol. I (1950), 135.

47 Ibid., Vol. IX (1962), 6.

48 Ibid., 16f.

III: The Elimination of the Jews

1 Gerald Reitlinger, *The Final Solution* (1953).

2 Eva G. Reichmann, *Hostages of Civilization: The*

Social Sources of National Socialist Anti-Semitism (1951) (German translation by the author, *Die Flucht in den Hass* [n.d.,1956]).

3 See above, Chapter I, notes 22 and 23.

4 Ernst Deuerlein (ed.), "Hitlers Eintritt in die Politik und die Reichswehr," in: *VfZG* 7 (1959), 185 and 204. Cf. Ernst Nolte, *Der Faschismus in seiner Epoche* (1963), 389f. and 444.

5 *Mein Kampf,* 20 (29); cf. Chapter I. fn. 1.

6 Nolte, op. cit., 408 (English translation, pp. 332f.) I do not completely agree with Nolte's interpretation of Hitler's antisemitism, as will become obvious below; on this interpretation cf. also the critique of Shaul Esh, "Eine neue literarische Quelle Hitlers?," in: *Geschichte in Wissenschaft und Unterricht* 15 (1964), 487ff.

7 Cf. Reginald H. Phelps (ed.), "Hitler als Parteiredner im Jahre 1920", in: *VfZG* 11 (1963), 274ff. The remarks below are based on the records of the *NSDAP-Hauptarchiv* now held by the *Bundesarchiv* of the Federal Republic of Germany in Koblenz, quoted below as *Bundesarchiv.*

8 *Bundesarchiv* NS 26/81-82, NR. 20; cf. also Phelps, op. cit., 277f.

9 Typewritten manuscript of 33 pages, with handwritten corrections which may possibly be Hitler's own; *Bundesarchiv* NS 26/62. Cf. Phelps, op.cit., 280 and 308f. This speech was published after the completion of this study with a commentary by Reginald H. Phelps (ed.), "Hitlers 'grundlegende' Rede über den Antisemitismus," in: *VfZG* 16 (1968), 390ff.

10 The reference is, of course, to the First Book of Moses, 3, 19.

11 These quotations are taken from an article by Hitler in the *Völkische Beobachter,* January 1, 1921, entitled "Der völkische Gedanke und die Partei," typewritten manuscript, *Bundesarchiv* NS 26/46; published (with an erroneous dating for 1922 and with copying mistakes) in Hans-Adolf Jacobsen and Werner Jochmann (eds.), *Ausgewählte Dokumente zur Geschichte des Nationalsozialismus 1933–1945* (1961ff.)

Notes

12   Article entitled "Rathenau and Sancho Pansa,"
     manuscript, *Bundesarchiv* NS 26/46, 19.
13   Heinz Preiss (ed.), *Adolf Hitler in Franken. Reden
     aus der Kampfzeit* (1939), 15.
14   See below, Chapter V.
15   *Mein Kampf*, 69 and 59 (83 and 72).
16   Ibid., 225 (269). When read in this context, the
     little word "now" — deleted later, probably for
     stylistic reasons — may well take on a meaning be-
     yond that of a mere expletive.
17   Ibid. Later editions have, more appropriately, "mil-
     lions of years".
18   Ibid., 69f. (84).
19   Ibid., 703 (906).
20   See above, p. 38.
21   *Mein Kampf*, 700 ff. (903ff.).
22   Ibid., 716 (922).
23   Ibid., 716 (923).
24   Ibid., 720f. (927f.).
25   Ibid., 724 (928, 931).
26   Hitler's estimation of the statesmen of Vichy
     France was quite similar. He showed respect for
     Marshal Pétain, who always delayed in the face of
     German demands; for Pierre Laval, however, who
     was ready to concede much more, Hitler held a
     deep-seated aversion. The axioms of Hitler's policy
     towards France furnish an explanation. Hitler was
     puzzled that Laval seemed to offer things which ran
     against the best interests of France as Hitler saw
     them. Pétain fitted more easily into Hitler's image
     of France since his reluctance preserved French
     interests. Cf. Eberhard Jäckel, *Frankreich in Hitlers
     Europa* (1966).
27   Bormann note, published only in French and Eng-
     lish translations: *Le Testament politique de Hitler*,
     ed. by François Genoud (1959), 57, and *The Testa-
     ment of Adolf Hitler,* ed. by H.R. Trevor-Roper
     (1960), 30f. The German original of this book
     quotes from the original unpublished German text,
     with the kind permission of M. François Genoud.
     (Translator's note: The English translations of this
     text are my own.)
28   Published in the Leipzig news magazine *Der Na-*

131

tionalsozialist, 1. Jg., No. 29, August 17, 1924; now available in the Bibliothek für Zeitgeschichte Stuttgart, Flugblattsammlung, Karton: Deutschland IV; Innenpolitik, Parteien: NSDAP.

29 *Mein Kampf,* 155 and 141 (185f. and 166).

30 Ibid., 280 (349). This passage should be related not only to the practice of so-called euthanasia during World War II, but also to Hitler's order, predated to September 1, 1939, "to expand the authority of doctors, to be named individually, so as to permit mercy killings of people who are, to the best of human knowledge, incurably ill and whose condition has been most critically determined." Nuremberg Documents PS-630 (German edition), *Der Prozess gegen die Hauptkriegsverbrecher vor dem Internationalen Militärgerichtshof,* Volume XXVI (1947), 169.

31 *Mein Kampf,* 610f. (800).

32 Ibid., 61,62,135,165,212,331,334,339,358 (75,76, 160,196,251,416,419f., 427,451).

33 Ibid., 310 and 359 (388 and 453).

34 Ibid., 185f. (219f.).

35 Ibid., 195f. (229f.).

36 Ibid., 738 (946f.).

37 Ibid., 772 (984).

38 This is Reitlinger's conjecture, op.cit. (1956), 137, at the beginning of a chapter dealing with the gas chambers. On their origins, cf. *Kommandant in Auschwitz, Autobiographische Aufzeichnungen von Rudolf Höss* (1958), 153ff.; on the prehistory of the gas chambers in the context of the so-called Euthanasia Program, cf. *Medizin ohne Menschlichkeit,* ed. by Alexander Mitscherlich and Fred Mielke (1949; new edition 1960), 183ff. A detailed study of the genesis of the idea of mass murder by poison gas would be desirable.

39 *Stenographische Berichte des Reichstags* (1939), 16 (B); (Stenographic transcripts of the Reichstag sessions).

40 Cf. Jäckel, op.cit., 53 and 225.

41 On all the details, cf. Reitlinger, op.cit., and Raul Hilberg, *The Destruction of the European Jews* (1961).

132

42   Speech in Munich's *Löwenbräukeller;* see *Keesings Archiv der Gegenwart* (1940), 4766.

43   Ibid., (1942), 5338; also in Max Domarus (ed.), *Hitler. Reden und Proklamationen 1932-1945,* Vol. II (1963), 1821.

44   *Keesings Archiv,* op.cit., 5379; cf. Domarus, op.cit., 1829.

45   Message on the Anniversary of the Promulgation of the Party Program, *Keesings Archiv,* op.cit., 5409; cf. Domarus, op.cit., 1844. A short time later Goebbels wrote in his diary (March 27, 1942): "The prophecy which the Fuehrer made about them [the Jews] for having brought on a new world war is beginning to come true in a most terrible manner." Louis P. Lochner (ed.), *Goebbels Tagebücher* (1948), 142. [English translation: Louis P. Lochner, tr. and ed., *The Goebbels Diaries,* (1948), 103].

46   Speech delivered in Berlin's Sportpalast: *Keesings Archiv,* op.cit. 5657; Domarus, op.cit., 1920.

47   Speech delivered in Munich's Löwenbräukeller: *Keesings Archiv,* op.cit., 5705; Domarus, op.cit., 1937.

48   Bormann note, cf. note 27 above; ibid., 86 (French translation) or 57 (English translation).

49   Ibid., 78,132,143, and 148; or: 50,95,105, and 109. Specific mention should be made of the note, dated February 13, 1945, which contains a final, retrospective summary of Hitler's antisemitism.

50   Nuremberg Documents (German edition), Streicher-9, *Der Prozess gegen die Hauptkriegsverbrecher,* op.cit., Vol. XLI, 549 and 552.

IV: The State as a Means to an End

1   *Mein Kampf,* 420f. (579); cf. above, Chapter I, note 1.

2   It has been printed in so many places that it will suffice here to enumerate its various points.

3   Thus in an additional preamble, added after 1933, in which it was stated: "All legal prescriptions have to be applied in the spirit of the Party Program." *Nationalsozialistisches Jahrbuch* (1941), ed. by Robert Ley, 153.

4 See above, p. 29f. On the later policy concerning the South Tryol, cf. Conrad F. Latour, *Südtirol und die Achse Berlin-Rom 1938-1945* (1962).

5 Cf. Troels Fink, *Geschichte des schleswigschen Grenzlandes* (1958), 298ff.

6 See above, p. 50.

7 *Mein Kampf,* 232 (287).

8 Cf. Heinrich Uhlig, *Die Warenhäuser im Dritten Reich* (1956).

9 Georg Franz-Willing, *Die Hitlerbewegung. Der Ursprung 1919 bis 1922* (1962), 79. On Drexler, cf. also Reginald H. Phelps, "Anton Drexler – Der Gründer der NSDAP", in: *Deutsche Rundschau* 87 (1961), 1134ff.

10 Werner Maser, *Die Frühgeschichte der NSDAP. Hitlers Weg bis 1924* (1965), 208.

11 Franz-Willing, op.cit., 68ff. and 79; Maser, op.cit., 176.

12 *Mein Kampf,* 423f. (680f.); the last sentence is emphasized in print by italics.

13 Ibid., 511-514 (680-683).

14 Ibid., 424 (583).

15 See above, pp. 14f.

16 On this subject, cf. still Ernst Fraenkel, *The Dual State* (1941).

17 Ernst Rudolf Huber, *Verfassungsrecht des Grossdeutschen Reiches* (2nd edition, 1939).

18 *Mein Kampf,* 380 (480).

19 Ibid., 433 (594); cf. 431 (592).

20 Ibid., 434 (595).

21 Ibid., 439 (601).

22 *Hitlers Zweites Buch,* 70 (English translation: 34); cf. also 62 (24). Other parts of this book will be used in the subsequent chapter. [Translator's note: For full title and use of the English translation, see above, Chapter II, notes 26 and 38.]

23 *Mein Kampf,* 151f. (178f.).

24 Cf. generally Gustav Stolper, *Deutsche Wirtschaft seit 1870* (expanded new edition, 1964) and the literature cited there.

25 *Mein Kampf,* 228 (281).

26 Ibid., 579 (764f.).

27 Translator's note: After the Reichstag fire, the

newly elected Reichstag was opened with a solemn act of state in the Garnisonkirche in Potsdam, March 21, 1933. With that act, the Nazis intended to present themselves as the legitimate heirs of the traditions of Prussia.

28 To have pointed out this aspect is one of the special merits of the book by Hans Bernd Gisevius, *Adolf Hitler. Versuch einer Deutung* (1963); cf., for instance, 202f. and *passim*.

29 *Mein Kampf,* 369f. (465f.).

30 Ibid., 374 (473).

31 Ibid., 368 (463).

32 Ibid., 374f. (473f.).

33 This quotation is taken from Heinz Josef Varain's unpublished inaugural lecture, given at the University of Giessen on January 30, 1968, entitled "Sozialismus und Sozialpolitik in Adolf Hitlers *Mein Kampf.*" The author wants to express his deeply felt gratitude to Mr. Varain once again, not only for the loan of his manuscript, but also – and especially – for the almost countless nocturnal conversations concerning the entire range of problems involved in this present study.

34 *Mein Kampf,* 416–418 (574–575); cf. also 397 (501). On Rosenberg's standard book *Der Mythus des 20.Jahrhunderts* (1930), which – in contrast to Hitler's *Mein Kampf* – gave rise to a heated literary controversy, Hitler commented (April 11, 1942) that he had "read it only in small parts since it was, in his opinion, written in a style too difficult to understand." Henry Picker, *Hitlers Tischgespräche im Führerhauptquartier 1941–1942* (1963), 270.

35 This question of the Führer principle within the Party resulted in 1930 in "the only substantive revision of an entire section" of *Mein Kampf;* cf. Hermann Hammer, "Die deutschen Ausgaben von Hitlers *Mein Kampf*", in: *VfZG* 4 (1956), 171f.

36 To avoid any misunderstandings, I want to emphasize that these remarks express, of course, nothing on the subjects of the historical and political preconditions of National Socialism or of the complex issue of responsibility, subjects which are of the utmost importance, but entirely different in kind

and thus not within the limitations of this present study.

37 The question whether there were any drafts is hard to answer and, unfortunately, completely unresolved. Werner Maser's book, *Hitlers Mein Kampf* (2nd edition, 1966), contributes — one notes with regret — virtually nothing to this question or to the subject as such, despite its subtitle *Entstehung, Aufbau, Stil – Änderungen, Quellen, Quellenwert – kommentierte Auszüge.* (In English this reads: "Origins, Organization, Style – Alterations, Sources, Source Value – Commentary on Excerpts".)

38 Cf. above, Chapter IV, note 22.

39 These passages will be treated in detail in the last chapter below.

40 See above, pp. 35f. and note 26.

V: The View of History as a Synthesis

1 *Mein Kampf,* 8 (15); see above Chapter I, note 1. Cf. also the autobiographical remarks on history as a favorite subject in school, loc. cit. and 11ff. (17ff.). On Hitler's aversion against "professorial teaching and understanding of History" and mere "repetition of external facts," cf. also *Mein Kampf,* 158, 320, 468, and 473 (188, 401, 630, and 635).

2 Ibid., 12 (18).

3 Ibid., 14 (23).

4 Ibid., 467 (628); thus also *Hitlers Zweites Buch,* 46 (5). See above, Chapter II, notes 26 and 38.

5 *Zweites Buch,* 47 (7).

6 Ibid.; cf. *Mein Kampf,* 468 (629).

7 *Mein Kampf,* 129 (152).

8 *Zweites Buch,* 46 (5).

9 *Mein Kampf* 324 (406).

10 Ibid., 372 (470).

11 The English translation of the *Communist Manifesto* is taken from the authorized English version, published by International Publishers (1964), 9. – Translator's note.

12 *Mein Kampf,* 319 (399f.) [Translators note: English word order made necessary minor inclusions

not in the German text; the sense of the quotation remains unchanged.]

13 For this and the following quotations, see ibid., 311–313 (389–392).

14 Ibid., 318ff. (398ff.).

15 Cf. Hans-Günter Zmarzlik, "Der Sozialdarwinismus in Deutschland als geschichtliches Problem", in: *VfZG* 11 (1963), 246ff. The comprehensive investigation of this topic promised by Zmarzlik has, unfortunately, not yet appeared in print. It should be emphasized once more at this point that the present study does not regard it as its task to search for the precursors and prefigurations of Hitler's *Weltanschauung.*

16 Cf. above, Chapter V, note 9.

17 *Mein Kampf,* 148 (175).

18 Ibid., 165 (197); cf. also 166, 233f., 316, 324ff., 366f., and 453 (198f., 288f., 396, 406ff., 460f., and 614f.).

19 Ibid., 275f. (343).

20 *Zweites Buch,* 46f. (5).

21 *Mein Kampf,* 312 (391); cf. also 325 (407).

22 Cf. Karl Lange, "Der Terminus 'Lebensraum' in Hitlers *Mein Kampf,*" in: *VfZG* 13 (1965), 426ff. While Lange quite rightly corrects the mistaken notion that this term had not been used in *Mein Kampf,* he surprisingly overlooks himself that it also occurs repeatedly in the first volume of *Mein Kampf,* thus e.g. 148, 164, 316, 333 (twice), and 334; (174, 195, 196, 396, 418 (twice), and 419f.). [Translator's note: The English translation does not always use the term "living space"; thus we read simply "space" (195), "living area" (196), and "living quarters" (419f.)]. This disagreement on such a simple and minor question of terminology indicates that historical research has still not sufficiently penetrated Hitler's book.

23 Thus even nomads and Jews had their own living space in Hitler's terminology; cf. *Mein Kampf,* 333f. (418f.).

24 *Zweites Buch,* 47 (6).

25 *Mein Kampf,* 69 and 421, 312, and 317 (83 and 580, 390, and 397). It is readily apparent that here,

too, a Darwinian expression, the "survival of the fittest," lies behind Hitler's words and is oversimplified compared to its original meaning, although Hitler was by no means the first to do so.

26 Ibid., 372 (469); cf. also 384 (486).

27 Ibid., 316 (396).

28 Ibid., 422 (581); on the "free play of forces" cf. 570f., 573, and 577 (753f., 755, and 761).

29 Ibid., 422 (581).

30 Speech delivered in Erlangen to an audience of professors and students (November 13, 1930), in: Heinz Preiss (ed.), *Adolf Hitler in Franken. Reden aus der Kampfzeit* (1939), 171. Cf. Günter Moltmann, "Weltherrschaftsideen Hitlers," in: *Festschrift für Egmont Zechlin* (1961), 197ff.

31 *Mein Kampf,* 319f. (400).

32 *Zweites Buch,* 47 (7).

33 Ibid., 48ff. (7–12).

34 Ibid., 69 (32).

35 Ibid., 62 (24).

36 Cf. *Mein Kampf,* 144f. (169f.), and also *Zweites Buch,* 56f. (17f.).

37 *Mein Kampf,* 317 (397).

38 *Zweites Buch,* 66ff. (29ff.).

39 See, for instance, *Mein Kampf:* on racial value, 272 (339), on personality value, 492ff. (660ff.), and on the instinct for self-preservation, 315ff. (394ff.). But there are numerous other passages relevant to these concepts.

40 For this and the following quotations, see *Zweites Buch,* 64–66 (27–29).

41 Ibid., 66–68 (29–32).

42 Ibid., 68 (32); cf. also 106 (79).

43 Preiss, op.cit., 81.

44 Max Domarus (ed.), *Hitler. Reden und Proklamationen 1932–1945,* Vol. I (1962), 70ff.

45 See above, pp. 51ff.

46 Cf. *Mein Kampf,* 185, 213f., 234, 257, 265, 350, 393, 403, 420, 505, 528, and 616 (219, 253f., 289, 318f., 331, 440f., 494, 509, 578f., 674, 707, and 808) – to mention just some of the passages.

47 To give just a few examples: *Mein Kampf,* 54, 64, 66, 257, and 589 (66, 78, 80, 320f., and 775). On

the Jewish nature of Freemasonry, cf. 345 and 521
(433 and 699f.).
48 Ibid., 346 (435); cf. also 492 (660).
49 Ibid., 69, 149, and 314 (83, 176, and 393).
50 Ibid., 69 (83f.); similarly 307f. and 498 (386 and
666).
51 Ibid., 347 (435f.); cf. also the extensive statements
on "Jewish Democracy" in Chapter III of Volume I.
52 Ibid., 357 (449).
53 Ibid., 351 and 361 (442 and 454); cf. also 314,
315f., 367, and 438 (393, 394f., 462, and 599).
54 Ibid., 165, 253, 333, and 335-337 (196f., 313,
418, and 420-424).
55 Thus again and again, ibid., 329-346 (412-435)
and *passim*.
56 Ibid., 342 (430); cf. 346 (434).
57 Ibid., 165 (196).
58 Ibid., 331 (416); cf. also 332f. and 334 (417f. and
418f.).
59 *Zweites Buch*, 220f. (211-213); the following
quotations are from these pages.
60 *Mein Kampf*, 70 (84).
61 *Zweites Buch*, 223 (215f.). Hitler repeated in this
context also his linking of antisemitic and foreign
policy arguments which we already encountered in
Mein Kampf; see above, pp. 54ff.

VI: From the Ordinary to the Extraordinary

1 *Mein Kampf*, 3 (7); cf. above, Chapter I, note 1.
2 Ibid., 8 (15).
3 Ibid., 20f. (29f.).
4 Ibid., 35 (45).
5 Ibid., 53 (65).
6 Ibid., 80 (95).
7 Ibid., 136f. (161f.).
8 Ibid., 138f. (164).
9 See above, pp. 34f.
10 *Mein Kampf*, 170 (202).
11 Ibid., 171 (203).
12 Ibid., 183 (216).
13 See above, p. 59.

14 *Mein Kampf,* 192 (226).
15 Ibid., 206 (244).
16 Ibid., 225 (269); cf. ibid., 242 (299).
17 Ibid., 239 (296).
18 Ibid., 71 (85).
19 Cf. especially Franz Jetzinger, *Hitlers Jugend* (1956). See also William A. Jenks, *Vienna and the Young Hitler* (1960).
20 *Mein Kampf,* 71f. (85f.).
21 Ibid., 73 (87).
22 Ibid., 72 (86).
23 Ibid., 11 (17).
24 Ibid., 244 (301).
25 Ibid., 406 (514).
26 Werner Maser, *Hitlers Mein Kampf* (2nd edition, 1966), 37; cf. above, Chapter IV, note 36.
27 *Bundesarchiv* NS 26/49 and 50; cf. as an example illustration graph 6 in Maser, op.cit., preceding p. 97.
28 The autobiography offers, nevertheless, several possibilities for a psychological interpretation, such as the one attempted by August Nitschke, for example, in his *Der Feind* (1964), 135ff. Although I do not agree with all the conclusions reached in that book, I would like to take this opportunity to thank my colleague, Professor Nitschke, sincerely for several suggestions and many instructive conversations.
29 Letter to Ernst Hepp, *Bundesarchiv* NS 26/4. Also quoted in *"Es spricht der Führer," 7 exemplarische Hitler-Reden,* ed. by Hildegard von Kotze and Helmut Krausnick (1966), 18. The final passages of the letter are reproduced on the cover of the German edition of this book.
30 *Mein Kampf,* 36 (47).